Love That Will Not Let Me Go

by

Lee Anne Worre Risk

Author's Note

This story has been a labor of love and has taken years to complete. It is my testimony of God's grace and faithfulness. I have told this story many times in many places. This book is a response to a constant stream of encouragement from those who heard it and were blessed. In the book of Revelations it says "They overcame by the Blood of the Lamb and the word of their testimony" We are called to be overcomers.

This book has been over two years in the writing. I am grateful to the many who prayed and all those who played a part and were used by God in beautiful ways that supported and blessed me. Many of those are characters in this grand play that the Lord Jesus directed and produced.

I want to acknowledge my dear brother, John Worre, who worked literally hundreds of hours to pull a pretty disjointed account into readable shape. Genny Kieley has become a real friend through our work together. Without her help, I fear we would still be wandering in the wilderness. This woman knows the ropes when it comes to bringing a book to publication.

When asked how I got through the trials that God gave me, I point towards heaven. What a wonderful God we serve. Amen?

Lee Anne Worre Risk

*This book
is Dedicated
to
My Lord
and to
My mother,
Pearl Jass
Worre*

Chapter 1

Central Mexico
April 28, 1988

People talk about premonitions. I believe that can happen. I know God can give you a warning – a kind of check or uneasy feeling in your spirit in order to direct you away from trouble or danger.

The day it happened I had no such feeling. For the past few weeks I had been carrying some heavy concerns that kept me feeling sad and a little afraid. We were preparing to leave Zacatecas, the city where we had been living. Zacatecas is in the central part of Mexico; a beautiful old city of pink quarry that holds magic, tradition and charm. It started out as a silver mining camp and is known as a "high place" for its elevation as well as religious significance.

We were heading up to the border. A road trip like this can be somewhat perilous. But the kind of thing that can happen traveling in Mexico was not something I felt I needed to worry about and was far back in my mind. Bad things happened, of course, but, as we all tend to think, those kinds of things would never happen to me. The ordinary, everyday risks one took when traveling by car through the open spaces between cities and towns were real, but not something I spent much time fretting over.

We were missionaries and Zacatecas was our home. We had started out fairly late in life compared to most, but had been serving the Lord for several years and were getting pretty used to the life. We loved it.

In today's world, Mexico can be truly dangerous – even to non-Mexicans, but that danger exists mostly around the border and in the port cities. Robbery, assault, kidnapping and many kinds of predatory villainy have become common. Though the drug cartels have been around for many years, they have elevated violence to a horrific level in some areas. Even back in 1988 though, you still stood a very good chance of encountering criminals. However, it happened most often out in the more remote areas, and we were well advised to stop for nothing. There were stories - true stories - about the bad guys putting women and children out in the road to make it appear as if they were in trouble and needed help. The Good Samaritans that pulled over to give assistance would find themselves at gunpoint and lucky to escape with their lives. Another warning we were given in our mission's training school was that we should not stop at what appeared to be the scene of an accident. The Mexicans knew that all us Americans carried auto insurance. If we stopped, they could lie about how we might have been involved and how we might even have been at fault. That scheme probably worked from time to time or there would not be those stories about repeated attempts.

We were old salts by then and knew just how most of this worked. Standard practice was to keep moving, start any trip with a full tank of gas and be sure you were in a well maintained vehicle. No worries on that score. Routine.

My concerns and the accompanying sadness were there, and I was looking forward to some kind of resolution to those concerns. I had a kind of ingenuous hope that this time on the road and the temporary change of scene might be the catalyst.

I got up early. I was an early riser on any typical day but had set my alarm just to be sure to have time to think everything through. I wanted to be able to get started soon to get there in daylight and an early start was a way to avoid some of the heat. I showered, brushed my teeth, applied a bit of deodorant, but no makeup; got dressed in traveling clothes, slacks and a plain blouse. Then, finishing up what I had begun the night before, did some serious and careful packing. The border between Mexico and the states was a full day's travel. Any trips to the border were always planned to take full advantage of all that needed to be done. That included shopping, updating our registration, etc. We were going to do as many of those things as we could. Then I would be continuing on to Minnesota by myself for some, hopefully, minor surgery. As the cliché goes, little did I know.

"Are you ready, Rory?" I shouted, expecting he would be within hearing.

"Yup. Just gotta find a couple of pairs of clean underwear," he answered from the far bedroom. I always thought calling a single item of underwear a pair was nonsensical, but English can be a strange language. A pair of socks? Sure. No nonsense there.

"Still in the laundry basket, honey," I called down the hall. "I didn't have time to put them in your dresser."

A pause. "Got 'em. Now I've got all I need. I'll double check before we lock up, though."

Typical man. Waits till the last minute and is almost sure to end up forgetting things. We had done quite a few trips like this, though, and repetition becomes habit. He probably did have all he needed.

We hauled our several pieces of luggage outside to the curb where our chariot awaited and we began to load up.

"This new truck is terrific for these trips," Rory said, as he fitted the last of our cargo into the back. He turned and gave me a smile as he slammed the rear door. That smile blessed me.

It was a beautiful day. Blue skies, almost white directly overhead with a few puffy clouds and not terribly hot. We drove carefully through the narrow streets and got out and past the so-called suburbs of our city. Parts of Mexico – the coasts – the mountains – are scenic wonders. Northern Mexico, however, once you are away from the coasts, is not that spectacular. Our beginning route to the border was up high in the mountains; the pretty part. We had a glorious view for a short time but soon were down to that central area. From there on we had a steady visual diet of rocks and sand broken by scrubby sagebrush and the omnipresent cactus. It was spring according to the calendar, but well before rainy season would start so today's view was one of monotonous brown, tan and gray. It would not start to green up again until mid-June, at the soonest.

We got in and got settled. No seat belt laws in Mexico so we could stretch out unconfined. I relaxed in the comfort of our new 3/4 ton Chevrolet Suburban; a truck, in the truest sense of the word, but fancier and made to carry multiple passengers. We loved it. Prior to this, we had always had diesel powered vehicles. Loud and smelly and never much for amenities. The Suburban rode a little stiff being a truck, but had nice upholstery and air conditioning. Before this upgrade in vehicular transport, we usually rode with the windows down when driving during the daytime; the sun-scorched air blowing through and cooling us by evaporation. Perspiration was a constant. It was important to drink lots of water to make up for the continual and steady loss of body fluid. A person could sweat themselves into dangerous dehydration. The air out in the country smelled dry and dusty. Inside now, with windows closed and cool, air-conditioned air flowing through, the ride would be "no sweat." The Suburban also had Cruise Control, a luxury option for us. Cruise control can give you a rest from trying to maintain the speed limit, but, on the other hand, can also reduce the amount of attention given to the serious business of piloting a two-ton vehicle at high speed; especially if you are new to the technology.

It was a good day with good things planned ahead. We were going to be using this trip to celebrate our wedding anniversary.

I looked over at my Rory. Rory was a good looking guy. Dark wavy hair, naturally ruddy complexion, nice brown eyes with a straight nose and a roundish face. A wonderful husband, a good dad to our three children and a great partner in the Lord's work. The Mexican people loved this sturdy gringo and his mentoring was producing the kind of "fruit that remains". My gaze lingered on his strong tanned hands gripping the wheel with confidence. Nice hands, too.

"Do you think the kids will be all right?" he asked me again.

"Oh, yeah. Our friends will keep a good eye on them while we're gone. They'll be fine," I replied. "We've got good kids."

"I know. We do. It's nice to have the kind of friends that step in and help like that," he said. "I used to worry that they'd suffer from being down here away from all the benefits back in the states, but they really do love it. Lots of friends and home schooling is going good."

"How do you like it?" I asked.

He looked over, a quizzical expression on his face.

"The truck; this Suburban. How is it to drive?"

"I like it," he replied, straightening out his arms and gripping the steering wheel. "It feels solid and sure-footed. I really like the way it handles" He reached out and patted the dashboard affectionately. He pushed the little button on the end of the turn signal to set the cruise control and looked over to see if I noticed as he took his foot off the gas pedal. He stretched and relaxed in his seat with an exaggerated sigh of contentment. "There we go. Now we can lean back and take a little nap if we want to."

"Very funny," I said. We had both heard of people misunderstanding the cruise control technology and doing that very thing. Funny, and tragic at the same time.

We drove on, not speaking too much. After being married that long, small talk was not very necessary and you could have periods of comfortable silence. In the last few months though, there had been a perceptible change in Rory's demeanor. He talked less, seemed preoccupied and a little distracted. During that same time, he seemed prone to periods of anxiety and agitation. I thought it must have to do with something he was going through and felt like this trip might bring all of it out. I tried not to be afraid of the possibility that there was anything going on that might hurt us. In a life that often seemed chaotic, there was one constant. My God was in control…always. Sometimes I had to remind myself of that comforting fact, but when I did, it always gave me His peace.

After an hour or so, I shifted a bit, stretched out my legs, lay back to one side and put them in his lap so I could nap. The truck had a bench-style front seat and so there would be no need for adjusting of an individual captain's chair. We stopped for gas and stretched our legs, then got back on the road. Our progress would be slowed from time to time as we encountered other vehicles making their way down the road. Motorized transportation in Mexico can be unusual. Mexicans keep their cars and trucks going for decades longer than Americans would ever do. The only time one would be taken out of service was if it was damaged to the point of being unrecognizable. Some of our visitors would look longingly at fifty year old Chevys still in use and seemingly in classic shape. Once given a close look, however, the classic part was only in the outward appearance, and looked good only if enough distance was between the car and the observer. Body putty and cheap paint created the illusion of quality. Reality was something else. We would come up behind an ancient sedan with wheels wobbling and smoke pouring out behind and have to take care to pass them without getting into trouble. A common sight was tired old pickup trucks with their boxes filled to overflowing with – not cargo – but people. People of all ages and sizes. Back then, you could come across the clichéd – burros. Sometimes ridden, sometimes pulling a cart. Burros and sombreros. Mexican emblems.

We drove through a few little towns, slowing while near houses, people and dogs. Our passing was always noticed and Mexican eyes followed us as we went by; some curious, some suspicious, some envious.

Awake now, I put my feet back on the floor and was sitting toward the window. Rory patted the seat next to him. That was his regular way of telling me to sit close. I, happily, did so. That's when Rory began to talk. At his tone, I quickly went on full alert.

"Lee Anne," he said, "I am so sorry for the way I've been acting." He began to weep. "I've been foolish and kind of crazy, I think. But I'm going to be better."

I sat stock still, looking at him from the corner of my eye, seeing tears streaming down his cheeks. I was suddenly fearful of doing or saying something that would distract or make him change his mind about what he was saying. *Is this what I've been praying for, Lord? Is the nightmare over?* I said nothing.

He kept on talking and crying. "I hope you can forgive me, Lee Anne. If you will, everything is going to be fine from now on."

I found my voice. "I love you, Rory. I forgive you totally. This is so wonderful to hear. We've all been so sad and confused. This will be such great news for the kids."

We talked a bit longer about our plans for the future. Happy talk. We had been approached to take over a mission in Japan and we were praying about how God would work that all out. Rory went quiet again for a minute. Then he looked over at me and said, "I have made this past year so hard on you. I promise that your life is going to be all "downhill" from now on." I knew what he meant. He wasn't saying we'd be going downhill. He was saying that we wouldn't be struggling through an uphill battle anymore. I smiled through teary eyes. My heart was rejoicing. Rory seemed at peace. I felt like my husband had been away and now was back. I rested.

Chapter 2

The road to the border was pretty flat; smooth, by

Mexican standards. Back then there were no shoulders and the side of the road could be anywhere from two inches to a foot below the edge of the asphalt. Nearer to the border, the road began to be cut by ditches; dry creek beds they called arroyos. That made it necessary to build little bridges. Those bridges added some bumps to the ride. The surrounding countryside got rougher. We came out of the flat lands into a hilly area where deep ravines fell off to one side of the road or the other. Foolishly, we were still not using our seat belts.

I was dozing comfortably when I felt a huge bump that jolted the truck. I was shocked when my eyes flew open and I sat up to see that we were off the road and heading directly for a concrete bridge abutment at a speeding rate. Without conscious intent, the word "Jesus" flew out of my mouth. Rory wrenched the wheel back on to the road to avoid hitting that immovable object head-on and we skidded past, missing it by inches. Now with the truck out of control, we slid and fish-tailed down the road and came to a near stop landing crossways to the road and on the edge of a precipitous chasm. That's when that luxury option we had been so thrilled to have took over. In all the action that had taken place up to that point, Rory, being a good Minnesota driver and knowing how to handle an out of control vehicle, had not touched the brake pedal. Most well-trained and experienced drivers have learned that when a vehicle at high speed has lost traction, it becomes a juggernaut that will continue in the direction in which it was heading. A less experienced driver will, almost always, hit the brakes hard, making the wheels useless in terms of gaining control. Steering into the skid makes the wheels still free to turn, then there is always a chance of pulling out. Cruise control is made safe by a touch on the brake pedal. That touch was not applied. The cruise control was still fully engaged and as soon as the tires could hold traction, our new Suburban did it's best to return to the 60 mile an hour pace for which it was programmed. Since we were facing that big ravine, that's where we headed.

At this point, Rory had probably hit the brakes but not in time to stop before we found ourselves careening down a steep embankment and being violently thrown around the inside of the truck. Rory was somewhat constrained by the steering wheel and held on to it with all his might. I was an unconstrained loose object and was being smashed and hammered into the sides, the roof and the dashboard. My face was cut and bloody and we had not yet come to a stop. Suddenly there was no crashing or banging or bumping – no noise at all. For a few seconds, we were airborne. Then we hit bottom. We hit so hard, the front axle (a piece of solid steel two inches thick) snapped. Rory had reached over to hold me back at the point of collision. His effort was well intended, but pretty much wasted. Our speed and the abrupt stop should have sent both of us through the windshield to our deaths. We were told later that it was a miracle in the truest sense of the word that we stayed in the truck. As it was, when we hit, the axle snapped and my back broke with a sound like a dry stick being broken over someone's knee.

I felt this major part of my body rupture and heard that sound. The feeling that went with it is hard to describe.

I have since learned that pain associated with damage to the spinal column will not always render a person unconscious. I can testify to that. If I had simply fainted or gone into a coma at that time, I would have been blessed indeed. Instead, I remained fully conscious and thus fully aware of a level of pain I couldn't have imagined any human could endure. I was crammed down under the dashboard and completely helpless to extricate myself. Amazingly, the doors still worked; not jammed shut from the impact. Rory, himself bleeding from a head wound, was able to get out of the car, come around to my side and pull me up. When he did that, I felt my spine separate. It felt as if I was literally broken in half. Once I was up, he positioned me so I could lie across the seat.

"LeeAnne, are you OK?

I couldn't speak.

"Can you hear me?" he said. "Are you all right? You're bleeding."

I groaned. "I don't know. I'm hurt pretty bad. I can't move. Something happened to my back."

The pain was so intense it was almost an audible sound. Like a scream. I was nearly crazy with pain. I have no memory of doing it, but Rory told me later that I just kept moaning "Jesus! Lord Jesus! Oh God, help me!" I do have a clear memory of that terrible pain

Then God answered and God signs began to appear. Out there on that lonely road where, up till then, we had encountered almost no traffic, a bus happened along. Though we were down in the ravine, we were not completely out of sight and someone spotted us. There were only about a dozen passengers, but they all came down to where we were to see if they could help in some way. The bus driver came to Rory and asked, in Spanish, of course, if there was something they could do.

"No, gracias, senor," Rory told him and indicated that more damage might be done if any attempt to move me was made. They stood in a hushed circle, but heeded Rory's warning and made no attempt to move me.

We all know you should never move anyone that has been injured till professionals arrive to take care of things correctly and safely. Why? You could get sued, is why. You might be accused of causing more damage. And, of course, that can even be true. What is that thing they say? "No good deed goes unpunished."

In Mexico, though, nobody knows those rules. Even if they had, there was no way of knowing how long it might take for those trained persons to arrive. No cell phones in those days, and no indication that the bus driver had a CB radio. In any case, maybe because Rory had been able to tell them they might hurt me worse by moving me, they stood around us but made no attempt to carry me up the side of the ravine. I think now they may have had a "God awareness" that this poor woman was being held in the hands of the Lord.

I was not very aware of anything but this driving, shrieking, universe- filling pain at that point. Besides the pain, I can only say I felt like I was in pieces; like there were parts of me that weren't connected to the rest. It seemed to me that my legs were twisted off to one side. I asked Rory if he could just straighten them out. "They are straight, LeeAnne," he said. That was when it began to sink in and I started to really understand what had happened to me. I lay there in the now unobstructed heat, with that solemn group of strangers circled around me and began to experience what enduring suffering was all about.

God sign number two. Earlier in the day, someone had been injured in another accident not far from where we were. An ambulance had been dispatched to take them to the hospital in the town a few miles ahead. He had delivered his patient and was returning to his own town when he just happened to come along the road we were on. The bus driver saw the ambulance coming, ran out into the road and flagged him down. Quickly explaining what had happened, he brought the ambulance driver down to where I was lying on the seat. That driver immediately took over. He carefully strapped me to a gurney, and they all helped carry me up to the ambulance. He had tried to drive it as close to the scene as possible, by coming down from the road to the side of the ravine. Then, with both Rory and I in the back, the driver continued on to his "home base", the little town of Concha del Oro.

Rory sat and held my hand, tears streaming down his face. He was miserable and distraught. He said the whole horrific event kept going over and over in his mind. He clearly felt responsible, accident or not, even though he, himself, was cut and bleeding and had suffered internal injuries. He either was not aware of those injuries or chose to ignore them. He may well have been suffering from shock as well.

I don't understand exactly why, but an ambulance ride is pretty rough – not at all comfortable. Maybe a vehicle that is built to carry everything an ambulance needs to have on board requires sturdy, stiff suspension. Most of the roads in Mexico are not as smooth and well- constructed as those to which we are accustomed. A rough riding vehicle and rough roads; not the greatest combination. Every bump felt like a hot poker being jabbed into my back adding further aggravation to the fracture of my spine. Under the circumstances, I was not complaining. I was suffering some added pain, certainly. Also, probably making some involuntary noises; but not complaining. I was in an ambulance and the ambulance was headed for a hospital. There would be doctors and nurses and pain killing drugs. I told myself that, surely, I would soon be fixed up and on the mend.

We pulled up to a little white concrete building and the ambulance attendant and Rory gingerly extracted this pain-wracked, moaning, very white gringa. I was covered with blood and had injuries not yet diagnosed, but apparently had been hurt badly.

"Something for pain, por favor," Rory shouted ahead. "Mi esposa, my wife is in terrible pain."

Lee Anne Worre Risk

It was not quite a hospital. In Mexico they have these little skeleton-staffed clinics in the more remote, less populated areas. They had no nurses, just some "helpers". There was one doctor on the premises. Well, not quite a doctor yet; a medical student. So, not quite a hospital and not quite a doctor. They had no narcotics. This was devastating news but something we should have expected, I guess. I found out later that due to the high likelihood of robbery, the little clinics only got drugs on demand and even then, just one dose at a time and always purchased by a family member off site. Those the clinic did get had to be brought from a larger *real* hospital or pharmacy. So even if someone was in dire need, they often stayed that way for several hours, at least. The strongest pain-killer they had available was a Mexican version of aspirin. Aspirin wasn't going to do much, was my thought, but I felt desperate for anything. They did have X-ray equipment.

X-ray tables are not padded. That's not a problem if you're not hurt. I was told to lay motionless for the picture to be taken. I held still, crying out in agony. One look at the developed film made it clear that the facilities they had in this little clinic were no match for the massive trauma I had suffered. I heard them use the Spanish word for "pulverized" in reference to my spine.

In the meantime, the *Federales*, the Mexican federal police, had arrived. They had come to arrest my husband and take him into custody. This was not quite as alarming as it sounds. Mexican law says the driver of a vehicle accident where someone is injured must be held for an investigation. The "doctor" told them that they could not take Rory away since he was the only one that could read my glucometer. They were surprisingly obedient. Many instances like this resulted in the police ignoring every circumstance and applying the law in a way that tolerated no interference. God was still in charge. There we were, in a medical facility with no one trained for something as basic as instruments that monitored blood sugar, but I knew a glucometer was all but unheard of in Mexico back then. I was glad, though. Rory would be with me. If they had taken him away, my whole outlook would have dimmed; glucometer notwithstanding.

I have Type 1 diabetes. I had found this out more than twenty years previous as a young girl and, at first, I was very frightened. I was told it could adversely affect my life expectancy and my ability to bear children. As time passed, I realized that diabetes was a disease that could be managed quite effectively. I just had to learn to get myself into the right regimen and watch my diet and my weight. Unfortunately, diet and weight control by themselves were not enough to deal with my version of this disease. Insulin injections were also necessary. Again, manageable. Leaving the US and living in a third world country was adding a level of risk that only made me rely more on the Lord. Insulin needs to be kept cool and in Mexico at that time, electricity could come and go. A lengthy power failure could make me very sick. But if God had sent me here, (and He had), He could keep me safe. But now…this.

Having been told they couldn't take the driver and hold him for the required investigation, the police agreed but decided to, at least, leave us under guard.

We were put in the clinic's storeroom. It was the only room in the clinic that could be locked. The room was small. Every wall was set up with either shelving or racks on which to hang things. Being just a storage room, no effort had been made to improve its appearance. The ubiquitous coat of whitewash had been applied haphazardly and ended at the point where they had been unable to reach further with the paint brush. One small window was set high in the outside wall. I was still on the gurney in which I had been delivered. They moved the gurney into that room and added a chair for Rory. Moving me from the emergency room was one more insult to my battered body, but they were as careful as they could be. Rory sat with me to wait for some kind of help – a real doctor, perhaps. Real medicine… please God!

Rory went out to find water. When he returned he told me about the guard they had placed outside the room.

"We've got protection, Lee Anne," he said. "I feel a lot better knowing there's an armed guard keeping an eye on us." He was being a little bit facetious, of course. He smiled. I looked at him. No one had paid him much attention with me being so badly hurt. He had not yet seen himself in a mirror. If he had, he would have tried to clean up a bit. He had been injured and the wounds were not tended to. The blood drying on his face made him look scary.

"It's a little Mexican guy. Maybe 120 pounds soaking wet. Cute old fellow. Got this big old pistol. Too big to put anywhere but across his lap. I'll bet that gun is at least 100 years old."

He was attempting to give me something other than my back to think about. It worked to some degree because that conversation stayed in my memory. Narcotics would have been better.

The night dragged on. Minutes seemed like hours.

For me, that night was a night of horror. Constant excruciating pain. Impossible to sleep. Diabetes can get wildly out of control in traumatic situations. Mine was going crazy. The danger was not as much from my sugar going too high, although that was not good, but if it dropped too low, it could put me in a coma and could even kill me. Rory sat with me and fed me the one medicine that can readily be found almost anywhere in the world; Coca Cola! Full of sugar (and in Mexico, real sugar – not corn syrup). It got into my system fast and kept me alive. I'm surprised the Coke people haven't picked up on this as, other than being carbonated and served cold, it is the one redeeming quality their product can boast. No…wait. Caffeine! Coke also has caffeine.

We spent the night praying, crying and wondering what in the world God had in mind.

At 5:00 AM, missionary friends arrived. They brought morphine. They tried to enter, but they were not allowed in. Now, looking back, I still find it hard to believe that there was actually some rule or regulation that kept us in and our medicine-bearing friends out. Three hours would pass during which we were acutely aware that the morphine was at hand. Three hours in the kind of misery that made it seem like three days.

At 8:00. I finally got relief when they let me have the morphine and it helped. Now, to get to the border.

Lee Anne Worre Risk

Chapter 4

April 29, 1988

One thing seemed critically important to everyone. I needed to get to a hospital that had the experience and personnel that could deal effectively with this kind of injury. That meant getting to the U.S.

Rory had been making calls to Zacatecas and to the family in the states. My sister Kathy was very involved in politics and she had contacts everywhere. Fortunately she reached out to our Minnesota senator and he got in touch with the Mexican ambassador. That helped expedite things.

Late that afternoon as they were preparing to move me to the airport, the Federales came back and took Rory away. They ended up keeping him for two days – far longer than necessary. They spent most of the time trying to convince Rory to sign over the Suburban to them. They had seen it from the top of the ravine, and it looked pretty good to them. It was obvious they had not gone down to check it as the doors wouldn't close. The miracle was that they had opened for us when we needed them to. The fact that they would no longer close and latch is, I'm told, a sure sign there was something very wrong with the frame. In fact, when they had a chance to examine it, the insurance people decided it was totaled.

Meanwhile the missionaries in Zacatecas scrambled to raise the funds needed to pay for an ambulance plane. I wish I could find out where all that money came from. I found out who a few of the sources were and have since been able to express my gratitude. It would be so great to talk to every contributor now and tell each of them what a blessing they were to us.

The ambulance plane flew from Guadalajara to Zacatecas to pick up a doctor friend of ours and my oldest daughter, Anissa. The pilot then flew to Saltillo where the Mexican ambulance crew along with our missionary friends carefully put Anissa and I aboard. Immediately, we took off for the border.

The pilot of that ambulance plane later told the doctor, "That was the roughest ride I have ever had!" The plane went through several air pockets and with each pocket, it dropped like a stone. If you have ever been on a plane encountering those kind of conditions, you know how that feels. The plane seems to free fall and then hits bottom so hard it seems like it's hitting the ground. Even in a commercial airliner, the experience is pretty terrifying.

The flight was not terribly long; probably an hour or so, but so rough that both the pilot and the doctor threw up. Pilots are usually pretty immune to airsickness, so this trip was clearly a corker. My daughter recalls that my gurney jumped six inches off the floor with every updraft and then slammed back down. Thankfully, the doctor had brought more morphine and had administered it to me as the plane took off. That ride was hard on everyone in the plane, but I was in my happy place and felt just fine. I always tell my students, "No a las drogas." *Just say no to drugs.* "But," I add, "when you truly need morphine, it is your friend."

When we neared the border, our pilot landed in Reynosa, just across from McAllen. That was as far as he could go. He did not have clearance to fly across the border into the United States. To the doctor and pilot's astonishment and to my daughter's horror, a hearse pulled up as close to the plane as possible.

"That's a car that carries dead people," Anissa exclaimed.

It was a black, slightly beat-up old Cadillac.

The woman who owned it heard her remark and responded, "Oh, yes, but this is also an ambulance. See the nice twirly light on the roof? We always wait till people die before using it as a hearse." Wonderful to know. Her son was the driver.

Anissa talked more with them and found out they were wonderful Christian people from across the border in McAllen, TX. When the request for an ambulance was made, of all those called, probably due to their unconventional equipment, these kind folks were the last on the list; probably because some folks might take a hearse ride as some kind of a bad omen. They also just happened to be the only ones willing to cross the border in the middle of the night.

They loaded me up and we drove back across the border. I was still pretty much "under the influence". We went straight to a hospital where the head of our mission and one of our fellow missionaries waited. Hospital staff immediately took me into the emergency room, and they began to work on me. By then, my respiration had fallen to a very low level and my heart was in trouble. Real trouble.

I was barely conscious as they labored over me, but I know I heard the doctor say, "We're losing her." Right then, I began the most profound and mystical experience of my life. I died. My spirit left my broken body and I was up above everything in the emergency room, looking back down at the doctors and nurses working on me. Free of pain. A spectator watching this tragic drama play out.

I wondered for a long time after that if I dreamed what happened next, or if that experience was a real encounter with God. Today I am certain the Lord was there with me. In a minute, I'll tell you why.

As I watched the scene from my vantage point above it all, I found myself willing and eager to leave this life entirely. For one thing, the people in that little clinic who attended to me after the accident hadn't even cleaned me up. There was nothing hopeful about how I looked. I was still covered with blood. For another, after the pain I had been forced to endure, it was easy to want to get away. I can remember thinking as I looked down at my body on the emergency room table, *"That broken person on the table* (although I knew it was me*) is a disaster."* Anissa later told me it was hard for her to believe that the tortured, battered person being taken out of the ambulance was her mother …I was unrecognizable still 18 hours later.

Then, all of a sudden, I was aware of Jesus' presence. I never really saw Him; I just knew that He was right there with me and that we were talking. It didn't seem strange to be in conversation with Him. That was probably due to the fact that the whole time since the accident, during every waking moment I had been speaking to Jesus. As I earlier related, my husband told me that for the first hours after the accident, all I did was call on God and Jesus, first one, then the other. It felt right also because my prayer life had always been kind of ongoing and conversational. I talk to Jesus about everything.

That being the case, as I looked down on the team of medical experts frantically working on me, it was like nothing had changed; at least nothing about my ongoing dialogue with my Savior and Lord. I was so grateful for how He had brought me through this horrific injury, that all I wanted to do was express that gratitude.

"Thank you, thank you, Lord," I remember saying. Then, because I had been in such terrible pain and looked a mess and because I was already out of my body anyway, I added, "Now, we can go." Pretty presumptuous, I guess. Better to have made that a question, huh?

"Oh, yes," said Jesus. "But not yet."

"Not yet?" I said. "Look at that. You want me to go back to that? "

Lots of Bible characters seem to have felt that it's okay to argue with the Lord. Look at Gideon, for example. That game he played with the fleece was a prime example. And Moses…and Jonah. Well, those people – big names in the Bible - had differences of opinion they felt free to present to God Almighty. Here's little Lee Anne to follow right along.

"Yes, child. It's not your time; not yet," He repeated.

Then He said something that got my attention off me and my mess and directed towards one of the most important things in the world to me.

"You have children," He said, "and your children need you." You might think he would have said something along the lines of "You have important things to do." He did not. He didn't have to say it that way. I knew my kids were important. He just said, "You have children." This was both a statement of fact, and as I would later learn, a promise for the future.

"Oh my goodness, I forgot all about my children," I said. "Of course, of course . . ."

That's when the emergency room personnel shocked my heart and brought me back.

* * *

A moment ago I said I would tell you about why I believe my experience of looking down on my body in the emergency room while talking with the Lord was not a dream. This is how I know it was real.

Two men—both friends of our family, were waiting with Anissa outside the emergency room door while that team of specialists fought for my life. Steve stood close to the door. He heard the doctor say, "We're losing her". He turned and called to our other friend, Dan, "The doctor just said they're losing her. She's dying."

Dan swore and hissed, "Don't say that!" knowing my daughter Anissa was nearby and not wanting her to hear.

No one ever told me about that exchange; but about three months later, Dan came to visit me in Minnesota. "Did you really say a swear word when Steve told you I was dying?" I asked him.

"You heard that?!" he stammered.

That conversation on which I had been eavesdropping took place in a waiting room totally separate from the emergency room. That's how I know for certain that I was out of my body, up above the action, watching and talking with the Lord.

I stayed there in that hospital for two days before being prepared for the trip north.

The local doctors' intentions were good, but they were doing things that a hospital should know not to do. There in Texas, they gave me milk and since I was paralyzed from the chest down, it was completely indigestible. When that became apparent, they put a tube down my throat and pumped my stomach. The gag reflex that process produced made my body twist and contort. That caused more of the most unimaginable pain. Dan, our missionary friend, who was there with me, pulled the tube out himself.

Chapter 5

May 1, 1988

A plane and pilot was found for the trip from the border to Minnesota. It was not an ambulance plane. It was a regular six-passenger Cessna. They removed the seats behind the pilot and Dan and Steve carefully installed me in place. I was still strapped to the gurney I had been carried on since leaving the little clinic right after the accident. It didn't fit into the plane well and had to be sort of jammed into place behind the pilot. Since the doctors there had not released me, they gave me no morphine when I left. I'll never understand that, but, possibly, it had to do with them being held responsible. I probably would have stayed there if the Minnesota doctors were not convinced that it would be bad for me to delay getting to a hospital where they could examine and treat me.

Everything was makeshift. Realizing I would be somewhat loosely contained, the boys strapped me in more securely using their own belts. They had put a frame-type brace on me. It was not very sophisticated, but may have provided some needed stability.

Some medical advice had been given over the phone regarding pain-killers. A long flight lay ahead and all they had for me was Ibuprofen. No more morphine to keep the pain at bay. We had to stop to refuel; a necessary delay, but we finally landed in St. Paul. One last ride in my brother's Suburban; a bouncy ride during which I was still kind of wishing to die; or at least, pass out. The doctor there commented that I had already bounced all over the country, so a little more couldn't hurt. If they had known a shard of bone was piercing my spinal column, I'm sure he would have been less cavalier. Finally, at last, I was in the hands of expert medical professionals.

I'm not sure at what exact point the questions began to form in my mind. I was badly injured – possibly facing paralysis, if not death. Like the old joke people make when they have been really sick; *"At first I was afraid I might die. Later I was afraid I might not."*

Why, God? I kept asking myself. *Am I not your child? I want to keep trusting you. Have I sinned? This surely feels like punishment. Is this the trial of my faith? Are "these things" going to work together for good?*

The word had gotten around and hundreds, if not thousands were praying and interceding. Was God ignoring their prayers? Where was the "good" in any part of this?

Chapter 6

Early childhood

I want the reader to get an idea of how my life was lived, growing up. My history is probably not that interesting or unusual, but the things that happened to me over those so-called "formative years" had God's fingerprints all over them. I'll be brief.

I was born in 1947 in a little hospital in Nebraska. We lived in a small town called Newman Grove; population around 800.

It was the time of nickel cokes and penny candy. Hamburger, .29 a pound. Bread, fifteen cents a loaf. Milk, delivered to your door every morning for twelve cents a quart. The war had ended a few years previous and it was, for some, a time of peaceful prosperity.

When I was born, we lived in a nice house on a quiet, tree-lined street. I was adored by two older brothers as well as by my mom and dad. Most of what I remember in pre-school years is triggered by old photographs. Standing in the family grouping, riding my first trike, typical camera poses. No painful memories at all.

We moved to Minnesota in 1950. By that time, the family fortunes had fallen and when we left, the house was nothing like the one I was born in. Only 50 or 60 years old at the time, but the only thing remotely modern about it was a tiny bathroom that had been built into a former pantry. It was relatively recent as evidenced by the outhouse still standing out in the back yard. I was too little to know the difference and enjoyed food, clothing and a roof as a matter of course. We were poor, but I had no idea. I was always smiling.

We were welcomed to my mom's sister's house in St. Paul. Housing, in general, was scarce. Almost no construction had gone on during the war. A lot of people were coming into the cities from the country looking for work. Those that had no family connections in the city were hard pressed to find places to live. Aunt Vi's was an old house, but big enough to hold us all as long as everyone was cheerful about sleeping arrangements. By the time every one was settled down for the night, getting up again for anything meant stepping carefully and lightly. I was a baby, so I don't remember.

Staying there was mortifying for my dad. It felt like charity to him, for one thing. Unemployment compensation, welfare, even favors from friends were abhorrent to this proud young man. The other thing that "got his goat" was that both mom and her sister Viola were on-fire believers. All that praying and Bible quoting, all that hallelujah stuff was a grinding irritant to a confirmed

Norwegian "man's man"! Religion was not, in his thinking, supposed to be part of people's daily life. He drank and he would still come home drunk, but he curbed the excess – something he wouldn't have been so concerned about if there weren't all those pious relatives to deal with.

Dad was so desperate to escape that when he heard about an alternative, he took it. He rented one of the strangest forms of housing imaginable. Some enterprising entrepreneur had purchased an assortment of railroad cars and set them up on cement block foundations in a sort of trailer park. The more affluent of our neighbors in that little development lived in the luxury of an entire car. That gave them a living space 8 feet wide and about 40 feet long. Our family was a bit envious of those, as we had one of the units that was half that size; one Pullman car divided into two apartments. You entered through a tiny front door, so small that even bringing in normal furniture was an impossibility. As you entered, you were immediately faced with a narrow door that opened to a miniature bathroom similar to those now found on airplanes. There was a letter in script on the door, which was the letter "L". Mom told me it stood for Lee Anne. That tickled me. We just happened to get the half of the pullman car that had the ladie's room. The main room that served as a combination kitchen, living, dining room, was about 8 feet square. Through that was the bedroom. When it was bedtime, that room was pretty much full.

Baby sister Kathy slept in a pulled-out dresser drawer. Big brother Johnny pulled up his knees to fit on the little divan in the main room. Rent: $35 a month.

I have actual memories of that time. When it rained the sound hitting the metal roof was so loud you couldn't hear yourself think. There were friends and we had toys. We were never hungry or cold. Our clothes weren't nice or new, but our neighbors were all in the same boat. Mom knew how to fix hair so starting back in Nebraska and through the rest of our lives at home, the sharp, unpleasant odor of permanent wave solution was, like God, omnipresent. We lived about a year in that tiny place before moving to the relative luxury of an actual house.

Chapter 7

School years were character building. We moved a lot and I had to change schools, find new friends and try to settle in every year or so. Once I got to the third grade, we kind of threw out an anchor. We had our own house. We took the downstairs level as it was an old duplex. My brothers slept in the basement and the upstairs family were our renters. There were lots of kids in the neighborhood and for the first time, school was only a few blocks away. Being able to stay in the same school with steady friends made life more normal; less embarrassing. Less embarrassing in most ways, anyway.

My little sister, Kathy and I walked to school which was several blocks away and trudged back home through the proverbial rain, sleet or snow for lunch. Most days I would simply heat up a can of soup and make us sandwiches. We had TV then; a big brown box with a little nine-inch screen topped with a rabbit ears antenna. You had to get up and go over to it to change channels and the changing knob was broken and gone. We were so pleased to have this entertaining status symbol that having to use a pair of pliers to change to a different channel became routine. There were only four choices anyway and three gave you a seeming endless snowstorm to peer through. The antenna was a key element in getting tolerable reception. You had to put it in an exact spot, and that spot seemed to move around on you. Dad had heard of a signal enhancer which he put into place. Tin foil wrapped around the ears in antlers and spears that actually seemed to help. Every day at 12:30, a soap opera came on – "As the World Turns" – and two little girls, Lee Anne and Kathy sat and closely watched that never ending drama. Back then, the stories were clean and decent. Kathy and I got very attached to the characters and it helped some with our being by ourselves so much.

My dad was a drunk. He drank every night and went on a binge once or twice a year. Binges were the only time he missed going to work; that was a point of pride for him. Kathy and I would be sent to the "beer joint" as mom called it, or to the liquor store, either in which dad would get comfortable and need to be reminded that family and dinner waited. I don't know if mom realized how uncomfortable those errands made us. I do think she hoped it would make dad feel guilty to have his little daughters come after him. I think it did.

In deference to dad's unpredictable behavior, we never brought friends to our house. Even when not bingeing, dad could be counted on to arrive home after work "three sheets to the wind". That's an old sailor's term. A sailing ship set up that way made no forward progress, but would simply go in circles. That arrival time varied based on how long it took to get too drunk to be served or for his money to run out. If we did not go out to find him and guilt him into coming home, we never knew exactly when to expect him. Every once in a while he would come home very late with a piece of beef steak to fry before he went to bed. It would usually be a big piece of round steak – the least expensive cut of anything that could be called steak. He would stagger around in our little kitchen and fry it up on the stove. He would begin to enjoy it and then feel guilty about having something so expensive all to himself. So he would wake all us kids up and we would stand next to him at the table like little birds while he fed us small bite after small bite. Mom didn't join us for those little feasts.

All my day-to-day friends lived within blocks of each other. They didn't bring it up, but they all saw dad weaving and staggering on his way home from time to time. That was embarrassing. He rarely drove drunk. That was a good thing.

There were pleasant memories too. My mother and her unfailing trust in the Lord were a cushion against the turmoil created by Dad's drinking and the occasional abuse he inflicted. As a family, we sang together whenever we took a car trip somewhere. Probably twice a year, we would get in the rusty old Chevy and drive the eight hours it took to go back down to Newman Grove. The radio never worked, and if you tried to read, you could get car-sick, so we would sing. One old hymn was a favorite and we learned to sing parts. Even dad would join us in his pleasant baritone.

When you walk with the Lord
In the light of His word
What a glory He sheds on the way.
When we do His good will
He abides with us still
And with all who will trust and obey.
Trust and obey
For there's no other way
To be happy in Jesus
But to trust and obey.

Thinking now about those words, it seems to be such a simple recipe to be happy in Jesus. When we were kids, they were just words. Now, I see the anointing in those words. Precious.

In my memory, it seems like yesterday. Mom and dad in front with baby sister Kathy in the middle. Me, snug in the back seat between my two big brothers.

The not-so-good memory is stopping by the side of the road and dad getting out, opening the trunk where he kept a bottle, and taking a snort before replacing it behind the spare tire. He would then get back behind the wheel and, fortified, continue on down the road. We all knew what was going on, but no one, not even mom, commented. The singing was stifled for a while, though.

We learned later that mom and dad had actually met singing in the choir at a Lutheran church on the east side of St. Paul. Our grandmother, Tillie, was the choir director. Grandpa Fred was a band-leader when mom was growing up. Even then, he loved to play the organ. That helps to explain mom's love of music. She was brought up in it. Now she was bringing us up the same way. She was instilling a love of music in us.

Growing up, I had a praying mother and an alcoholic father. It was no challenge to see the benefits of one over the other. Mom, though, was no quiet little church mouse. To any observer, she was what you had to call, a fanatic. She had been a "Beauty Operator" for almost all of her wedded life. She had customers that loved how she fixed hair and would go nowhere else. At first, as I mentioned earlier, she did her hairdressing at home. Once back in St. Paul, she spread her wings a bit and went to work in an actual salon. Since her main mission went past merely making money, she was confined as an employee so she rented half a barber shop and soon after, opened up her own business. That was located just a few blocks from where we lived on a store-lined street between a saloon and the neighborhood drugstore. Arcade street, it was called. Mom now had her own little ministry and named it aptly, if not terribly imaginatively, "Pearl's Beauty Arcade." She was now free to witness and talk about Jesus to anyone who entered her little establishment. Tracts littered every surface and the walls were hung with Bible verses and Christian slogans. When a customer looked up to see herself in the mirror, she was faced with bordering rows of scripture. Mom checked out sight lines and made sure there was no place in her shop where a Bible verse or a picture of Jesus was not visible; even from the shampoo sink where, due to a strategically placed mirror, The Word was clearly displayed. Mom was an unabashed "Jesus freak" well before it became fashionable. She sowed seed, soaked it with spiritual water and saw a harvest; first hand.

And Dad was a drunk. It's funny how kids think, though. On the one hand, dad was an embarrassment. On the other hand, Mom was as well. I wasn't too happy about any of my friends getting a close look at either of them and their respective antics.

I went to church, was involved in the youth group and had friends there. Most of those friends were also friends at school. We were saved; born-again kids, but not very evangelistic about it, if you know what I mean. As far as my Christian life went, God was off the throne in my life and I had climbed up there to take charge of nearly every decision. I knew I was saved. I was only three years old when it happened, but I remember so clearly asking Jesus into my heart and then skipping around the room with such a feeling of happiness. That experience was real and influenced me to lead my own kids to Jesus when they were little, as well. I just let Jesus as Lord get away from me during those teen years.

High school was a good time. I was involved in music and drama. I had the lead female role in "South Pacific". That was exhilarating. For a while, of course, I fantasized about a life in the theatre. Also, of course, I was no threat to the thousands of other Hollywood hopefuls. As I think about it now, I guess I must have been not too bad – acting and singing. After all, there were quite a few others that auditioned and they picked me. Maybe God gave that to me to give me a little self-confidence for what lay ahead.

Lee Anne Worre Risk

Chapter 8

June, 1965

Out of high school, the real world began to show its teeth. There was no free ride as far as financial support from my parents. My older brother had taken his wife and new baby to Detroit to manage a restaurant there. That position only lasted one year, but my brother stayed in the city to pursue other endeavors. A friend from Minnesota took over the restaurant and hired me to work as a hostess. My little sister and my best friend were my roommates. Once again, God was not at all in the forefront in my life. I was out and away from parental oversight, free to be me, as it were. It gave me the opportunity to be independent and to be able to do foolish things, which I proceeded to do.

I, somehow, got a pretty good job as a liaison for VIP patients who were being treated at the famous Henry Ford Hospital. My life style during that time was pretty worldly, but don't ever underestimate the power that is generated by a praying mother. I never could get totally away from the things of God. My whole life, up to that point, had been permeated with Jesus. Saved as a child.

Constantly fed a diet of scripture and prayer by a faithful and unrelenting mother. Out of habit or guilt, I went to church. I was in that no-mans-land so many nominal Christians find themselves. Not comfortable in a bar or in a prayer meeting. Went to both anyway, but couldn't get committed in either direction. I was owned but not operated by a loving Savior and Lord.

My work put me in proximity to young men who were on their way to Viet Nam. My heart went out to them. I really cared. I knew that in that terrible war, these guys were going to be in real danger. I wanted them to know the Lord. I wanted to share Jesus with them. Those kinds of thoughts were running through my mind all the time. I would try to screw up my courage to say something, but find myself tongue-tied and silent. I was frustrated. I couldn't understand why I was so powerless.

Like so many, I made resolutions, I set goals, I tried to read the Bible and pray. I was on that typical "self-help" program. I had been taught the truth; that Jesus in us is the only way to do or be anything of value, but it's amazing how proud the flesh can become. Like New Year's resolutions, every effort lasted for a brief time and then came to nothing. Where was my resolve – my backbone? Was I really so weak? Why couldn't I just be a better person? Well, of course, every born-again Christian knows why. In His love for me – for us, God will allow no attempt at self-justification to succeed.

By now, I was ready to do whatever was necessary to get my life in the right place and put Jesus back on my heart's throne. I just wasn't sure what that was.

June, 1969

My brother, Dennis, had been living a life far from God. He was smart and stubborn, his rebellious nature taking him down a pretty destructive path. He was bitter towards God but being a product of a Godly home and constant church attendance while growing up, he had enough education and head knowledge that he could take the average Christian and, using scripture, figuratively slap them silly and leave them standing there stunned and shaking their heads. He delighted in doing just that. At around this same time, he had gotten to the same point to which I had come. He finally saw the truth, that Jesus was the answer and we – brother and sister – began together to follow Jesus. We would spend hours talking about the Lord and what the Bible had to say. Soon after that, I returned to Minnesota.

I had had several somewhat serious boyfriends. None of those relationships had been enormously God-honoring. I was not totally worldly, but God was not in His rightful place very often.

In the glow of my new-found rebirth, I saw no need for the kind of emotional confusion a man can bring to a young girls life. I guess, at that time, I felt God wanted me single – kind of a protestant nun, as it were. There was plenty of advice in The Apostle Paul's letters that made the single life pretty sensible. Paul's remonstrations were mostly aimed at men, but it seemed like the same principles could apply to me.

My life became Christ-centered. I worked of course, but spent a lot of time in the study of God's word and in prayer and worship. There were meetings going on all over the place and, like my brother, I tried to get to all of them. Church was comfortably warm and the so-called "fellowship of the saints" became very real for me. Our gang of young fanatics did everything together and, inevitably, romantic attachments formed. Some of my friends were not convinced that my plans for a single life were what God had in mind. One night, one of the girls mentioned one of the guys.

"LeeAnne, you two would make a great couple!"

"Why? What's he like?"

"He's a football player, for one thing."

"I never go out with jocks," I said.

She told me more and things developed. That football player would eventually become my husband.

Chapter 9

Rory Risk was the son of a Lebanese father and a Swedish mother. Good looking and possessing an affable personality, Rory made friends easily and was, himself, a true friend. He was always loyal and supportive. Out of high school, he went into the service, but was given a medical discharge due to hypertension. That left him free to begin college.

We were both attending the University of Minnesota at the same time one year, but did not meet until the following year at Soul's Harbor, the church we both attended. I remember our conversation during that first meeting was about missions.

Rory was a steelworker; one of those that walked the girders on skyscrapers under construction. His co-workers called him "The Preacher." He had a bold witness. The more I got to know him, the more I saw how we fit. I fell totally in love.

Our wedding was beautiful and in my eyes, our marriage was perfect. I was pregnant soon and our first-born, Anissa, was a blessing followed in appropriate intervals by our son, Rory Jr., and our baby girl Katy. Three terrific kids that made our lives complete and fulfilled.

We worked, raised our family and time passed. For both of us, missions stayed on our hearts.

In the fall of 1975, my dad died. A year or so before that, after a life wasted in bitterness and alcohol, dad had finally given in to God. His Norwegian stubbornness coupled with what I now know as an unwillingness and inability to trust God kept him shackled to drink till cancer, literally, grabbed him by the throat. Cancer of the esophagus was pressing on a nerve that was out of the reach of surgery. At the same time it was growing in size and, slowly but surely, choking him and starving him to death. There was an attempt to go in and cut the nerve the growth was affecting, but that was unsuccessful. His pain was enormous and my brother was given some training so strong drugs could be administered by injection. Toward the end, he was no longer hospitalized. The drugs helped and it was wonderful to see my father praying and so obviously born again. When the pain would be at its worst, it would always succumb to prayer and praise. It was never gone for good, though. Not till he left and went to heaven. I like thinking about being with him when we all get together there. We went to see him on Katy's first birthday. She took her first steps that day with her Grandpa to see. He loved singing about Jesus, so we often got around his bed and sang. Kathy didn't want to try to sing soprano (probably because she was an alto) so I carried the melody. When Dad asked who sang soprano, I said it was me. He said it sounded so pretty. His last compliment for me, and really the only one I can ever remember him giving me. My dad went to be with Jesus that night. I know he was pleased that we came. I am grateful that we got there before he died.

Lee Anne Worre Risk

Chapter 10

God's call

There are people that are "called" to the mission field the same way too many are called to the ministry. They "feel" the calling just because it seems like interesting work. They also imagine the job to be not that difficult and they like the idea of being looked up to; respected. In addition, to the casual observer, ministers seem to live a decent life-style and seem to be taken care of financially. All in all, not a bad career choice.

The mission field also has an added element, that of danger. This, to many young people, adds a kind of exotic glamor. Romantic thoughts of living in a far country where American missionaries might be risking their very lives can be exciting and compelling to some young people; especially those who are enduring what they feel to be boring lives. Their lives at home just don't offer that kind of atmosphere. Foreign missions seem attractive due to stories heard of missionaries living in big houses with a staff of servants. Many denominations seem content to be supportive and provide relatively luxurious living conditions for those who serve in other countries despite scant results in terms of converts or students.

People "called" in that way are destined to live frustrated and fruitless lives, yet thousands "serve" congregations and foreign missions without any semblance of Godly direction or any sign of the Holy Spirit at work in their own lives. Their "gospel" is often limited to social issues with sermons and teaching devoid of any scriptural content. When the Bible is quoted, it is often to support one bland political position or another. It's kind of sad, but a reality.

I am glad that this is not the case with all American churches. We see many with fire for missions in their congregations and that send out new recruits every chance they get. I guess what I'm trying to get at is that God's calling when obeyed produces fruit. God's call was clear for our family.

Chapter 11

In 1979, our efforts intensified. We began to

assume some leadership in ministry as we developed what is often
called a "Cell" group in our home. That term is so appropriate. A
cell in a body. A tiny lively part of that universal Body of Christ. If
you have never been a part of that kind of fellowship, you have
missed out. Those meetings were amazing. Everyone hungry –
feeding on fellowship and the word. Regular food, too. Before
long, there were thirty couples filling our house for those weekly
Bible studies. Rory led those sessions. People found the Lord there
in our home. People grew in the knowledge of the Word. We saw
miracles of healing and deliverance. The supernatural was feeling
more natural all the time. We had one main weekly meeting, but
there was a steady stream of people coming and going, all week
long, day and night. We were being groomed by the Holy Spirit and
were learning more every day.

By 1980, we had gotten some sea legs. We felt certain of God's
call. Learning of our search for His direction, the head of our
missions board at church heard about a farm located west of the

Twin Cities that was available to rent. God had given him a vision for a missions training center and he wanted Rory and I to head it up. We had been advised that it would be good to have some knowledge of agriculture to take with us to a foreign country. This farm seemed ideal for the purpose.

The farm was just outside of a small town. We were only about an hour from the city so not that far from all our friends, but it was far enough to feel like we were "out there". The house and out-buildings were set back from the road with a few trees surrounding them. The land was flat with some swampy ground here and there. To us, it was the Garden of Eden.

Word traveled. Before long other young people responding to God's command to "Go" began to join us and we soon had a full complement of eager disciples. We re-configured the living space to make separate room and privacy for the girls.

The local townspeople gave a skeptical eye to the busy little bunch of apparent hippies and decided that we were up to no good. Rumors were flying.

"Somebody told me they're some weird kind of cult" was being said.

"There are big bags of marijuana seeds in the barn out there!"

Big bags of seeds, all right, but seeds for very standard crops like oats and alfalfa.

As time passed, the locals relaxed and began to tell their friends that we were nice people.

We were given very helpful information from the University of Minnesota. Rory actually attended classes on agriculture there for one semester. A wonderful missionary support ministry called Bethany Fellowship was an enormous resource. Back then, they were not so well known, but today Bethany is still focused on missions and has become quite renowned as an excellent Christian publisher.

Christ for the Nations, a missionary training school in Dallas, Texas, offered an extension course that added valuable fuel to the fire burning in our hearts.

People prayed; people gave. We were blessed.

Lee Anne Worre Risk

Chapter 12

1981

We got to the point where we could see no unmet need. Oh, there were a number of times when it was close and once or twice where, like those three Hebrew boys, we had to be rescued out of the fire, but God's promises are always kept. It was time. We felt ready to take the next step. All that support and the peace of God in our hearts just added to the faith and conviction with which we had begun. We were doing what we needed to do. We were on God's track.

Rory went on a missions outreach trip to the impoverished country of Haiti and took an excited and dedicated group of people along with him. This was an important part of our education. Haiti was truly a foreign land. Where many in the group saw the trip as a great experience – one to be remembered, Rory determined to pay close attention to every aspect of life in that relatively strange and hostile environment. He wanted to know how life worked in a country where everything Americans take for granted is either absent, or in short supply. He watched and took notes about all the little things. How did they keep the insects away from their food and themselves? What kind of protection was used against thieves and intruders? How did they store their food? He thought hard and asked questions about every area that we might face in our future mission field. The rest of the group would be going home to what was normal in the U.S. For them, this little adventure would be a great conversation starter with their friends and relatives. We, on the other hand, might actually be living this foreign life in some country, somewhere around the world. And we might be doing that soon.

We began to be in communication with various outreach organizations. One of those – PAOC – Pentecostal Assemblies of Canada looked us over and offered us a post in the Northwest Territories; a place called Yellow River. Our ministry there would be to the Indians and Eskimos indigenous to that area. We knew that extreme weather conditions were the norm in that part of the world, but that fact did not enter into our thinking. Rory was offered the position of hospital director. We prayed and kept ourselves open for Holy Spirit guidance. We made an exploratory trip, but did not go to the frozen north.

We were soon to discover that there are other extremes when it comes to weather. Cold is just one.

Chapter 13

God directed us to Mexico
1982

World Indigenous Missions, a group that does what the name implies, was pleased to have us join their ranks. Our mission was to spread the gospel and then to train and disciple native Mexicans to preach and pastor their own people. First step? One year of specialized training at a school right on the border. Spanish was taught, of course, but we were also given a thorough education in Mexican culture. We needed to become as familiar as possible with the customs and traditions of these people so as not to be seen as those "ugly Americans" we have all heard about. For example; you should never measure the height of a person – even a child – by holding your hand out palm down "about so high." That gesture was for horses. With people, you held a thumb up. And sarcasm, an American's favorite form of humor, was never to be used. Not at all funny, to them. Just confusing, and possibly irritating or offensive. What most Mexicans think is funny is the broadest form of slapstick. If you have ever watched Mexican television, you know just what I mean. What we learned was invaluable, but not all-inclusive. There would be many lessons learned "the hard way."

When God called us to be His servants in Mexico, we were excited – but also a little nervous. For children, learning a new language is relatively easy. For Rory and I, not easy at all. We knew we would have to have a good command of the Spanish language or we would have little chance of being productive for the Kingdom. After a year, we felt we were reasonably fluent and ready to go in. We had learned all 39 tenses of the Spanish verb and a huge amount of vocabulary in that year and as I think about it now, I am impressed. Once we were actually in action, we quickly got a few lessons in humility. It would be the Mexicans, themselves, who would become the kind of teachers that made things stick.

One time when we had to be away for a few days, Rory went to a neighbor to ask a favor. The neighbor was puzzled, at first, then laughed and explained to Rory that the favor he was asking was for him, the neighbor, to "eat my dog". What Rory was trying to ask, of course, was if the neighbor would feed the dog. No harm done, but there are, of course, plenty of true stories of dogs being eaten. In China, for example. Contrary to the urban myth, Mexicans don't eat dogs any more than you or I would. Lots of other unusual delicacies, but not dog.

Another young missionary worked very hard on his sermons. It is no small task to prepare a God-sent message in any situation, but taking what the Lord gives you and converting the content to a relatively strange language can be a real challenge. One day he was preaching and nervously laboring through a presentation of the gospel which had his audience completely enthralled. Then he began his invitation for those who felt God stirring them to step out and publicly declare their desire to dedicate or re-dedicate their lives to Jesus. As soon as he came to that part, his audience grew visibly uncomfortable. No one moved, but no one was willing to meet his gaze. At this point, he thought they were under heavy conviction and he repeated his appeal with more volume and intensity. Finally, his wife seated at the organ caught what he was saying and nearly fell off the bench in laughter. That was the cue for the congregation to follow her lead in uproarious glee. The harvest that night was sparse. The young fellow was completely confused. He stood there with a red face and a tentative smile until he, with his wife's help, realized what had happened. "You were doing really well", she said, "but when you gave the invitation, the words you used were, "If God is speaking to your heart and you know you need forgiveness for your sins, right now, get out of your seats, come forward and urinate (pee) on the altar!" He told people the story and always added; "It was a good thing it was my own flock" They, of course, never let him live it down. That tale has often been told since it happened. It was a good one. Other "faux pas" were fairly frequent, but not so embarrassing.

Lee Anne Worre Risk

My pastor brother, Dennis, enjoyed a service with us where the musicians played their usual exuberant brand of worship. One of them played the bass guitar. As he walked by, my brother tried to say something complimentary in what he imagined must be understandable Spanish.

"Bueno Basso," he said with a smile. What the young Mexican heard was "Bueno beso" which means "Good kiss." No harm done.

Chapter 14

May 1, 1983

Our first year was spent in the low country.

Translate that as hot; very hot! Especially, of course, in the summer, which always lasted about nine months. The place was called Ciudad Valles. This mission and time was designed, we joked, to make us grateful to be sent anywhere else in the world. If Mexico can be looked at as a body, Ciudad Valles must surely be the armpit. Temperatures were routinely around 110 degrees Fahrenheit and I have an indelible memory of one five day period where it was a constant 135 degrees. Add high humidity to that heat and you have a recipe for the ultimate in climatical (is that a word?) discomfort. As most people everywhere have heard, Mexicans; particularly those in the low areas, go and hide in the shade during the hottest time of the day. Siesta, they call it. So do we. It has almost become a word in English. Every store closes and people take naps. The only establishment that remains open is a single gas station. That is the law. It's no coincidence that the gas stations – PEMEX--are government owned.

This was primitive living. Rory had seen rough conditions in Haiti, but this was even rougher. We had electricity, but usually only for about five hours a day. Walls and windows were made of louvered slats; the main building material being cement blocks; painted, but just cement blocks, even for the partition walls that made the house into rooms. Ants – millions of ants – were everywhere and always. Rats the size of small dogs burrowed in and around the dirty little shack we called a house, making furtive forays into cupboards and trash. And the fabled cockroaches – "Las cucarachas" – were so big we joked about putting saddles on them. Unusual food; uncomfortable beds; sheets damp with humidity. Nights slightly cooler than daytime, but still so hot that our dreams were often dreams of fire. Uncivilized conditions in general… and yet we were so happy to be there. There was this enveloping sense of being in the center of God's will. There is no greater – no safer place to be.

Our ministry there in Ciudad Valles was to Mexican Indians. Ironically, we had spent a full year learning Spanish, a language these Indians did not understand. One language was called Nahuac, but there were actually dozens of languages spoken in those mountains. Rory preached, but invariably needed an interpreter. We saw people saved, but not very many. Satan had held these people captive for hundreds of years and was not at all willing to let them go. Witchcraft was the predominant opponent.

Many of the villages in which these people lived were up in the higher elevations. Some of them had never heard the name of Jesus before the missionaries that had preceded us had come. We thanked the Lord for those pioneers in ministry. We looked forward to those trips. Not only was every excursion a new adventure, but the temperature up there was better. We would load up our Suburban (and I do mean load up) with lots of water, a thermos of coffee and then head out. The roads were primitive. Narrow tracks with jungle vegetation crowding the edges. Hollywood portrays those kinds of roads and actually gets it right. We hung over the sides of mountains and our tires would be right at the very edges of deep precipices. On occasion, we would have to get out to remove rocks that had fallen down from the mountainside to block the road.

Often, we would be invited to eat with these people. In the mountains, the typical fare was not at all typical. There was a kind of root they ate which was impossible to bite off. Once you put it in your mouth, this long slimy thing had to be consumed. There was no option. You swallowed and swallowed till you got it down. Missionary kids learned to pray there would be no Coleman lanterns or other good light so they would not have to see what was in the food they were eating. Those good people did their best to offer us what, to them, was tasty stuff. Tasty stuff that would include different kinds of bugs, small animals, (I don't like to think about what kind, even now) and things they caught from the river that were best left unnamed. Tamales should never be anything but good, but, in the mountains, we called them "surprise bags" because as we unwrapped the banana leaves they were cooked in, we would find things we had not ever recognized as edibles. A piece of a pigs ear, for example, or a chicken foot. The mountain Indians were so pleased to be able to offer Rory and I a chicken foot. We would smile and enthuse over their idea of a delicacy and nibble dutifully while trying to avoid the toenails.

At the end of the evening it was not unusual to pack 30 people into the area behind the front seat of our truck as in each village our little flock would often ask if they could ride down the mountain with us to get closer to their homes. They had all walked long distances uphill to get to the meetings. Now they realized there was the possibility of a ride back home. How could we say "no". Group by group, family by family, they extricated themselves from the Suburban as we descended towards the city. It looked kind of comical with heads, arms and even legs sticking out of the windows. If you've been to Mexico, you have seen the way they maximize the space in their vehicles. That was us.

Our assigned task there was to start at least one new church and be sure there was a native Mexican Christian capable and called by God to pastor. Seasoned missionaries, Terry and Marilyn Day, returned from itinerating in the states and helped get it done.

We saw our first miracle there in Ciudad Valles. We had been invited to a wedding in the downtown area. We knew almost no one, but Terry and Marilyn had been there long enough to be thought of as wedding guests and we were going along with them. Actually, only Marilyn and myself were planning to attend since the men already had some kind of outing planned with a young Lebanese fellow. Terry was excited for the young man to meet Rory as he knew Rory had Lebanese blood. A fairly large number of people from the Middle East immigrated to Mexico in the 1940's. In fact our families' favorite ice cream shop was called El Acropolis. Catchy business name, wasn't it?

We were always comfortable leaving the younger kids with our oldest, Anissa. Terry and Marilyn had two tiny ones, but Anissa could care for them very ably.

Only one room in the house was air conditioned. That room was their office. It was not a very big room, but during the hottest weather, their whole family slept in that room on a mattress on the floor. We wanted all the kids to be comfortable, so we set them up in that office with crayons and paper and our boy, Rory, had his toy soldiers. We had no intention of being gone for long. As soon as the ceremony itself was over, we politely congratulated the newly married couple and excused ourselves from the reception party.

We got back to the kids just before the guys arrived. I was pretty dressed up, having even donned panty hose. I was unique in that regard, I'm pretty sure. The boys had been up in the mountains and were dressed in hiking attire and wore heavy combat-type boots. As soon as we got there, the kids all came tumbling out of the room to see us and ask about where we had been. My panty hose were killing me. They felt glued to my skin. I told the others I needed a minute and went into the air-conditioned office to rid myself of them. It took less than a minute and I was feeling real relief as I turned to come back out to join the others. As I did, I saw a huge scorpion scurry down the wall and scuttle behind their sofa. I screamed a nice lady-like scream and they all came running.

"A scorpion," I cried. "A big one! Behind the sofa!"

The men pulled the sofa back, exposing the ugly critter. This was Terry's house and he had already changed from his heavy boots into tennis shoes. He tried to kill it by stepping on it, but it was, indeed, a big one. It kept going. Rory leaped forward and stomped that venomous creature with his heavy boot. We heard the crunch. The scorpion was dead.

For me, that was such comforting evidence of God's protective care. Our kids had been there in that little room with an animal that could have killed one of them. More than that, Terry and Marilyn and those precious babies would have gone in to sleep with that nasty bug. An adult might survive a sting by a scorpion that size, but a baby would almost surely die

The number of converts was pretty small. The little church was up and going, though, so we were told we should get ready to be reassigned.

When we left Ciudad Valles, we did so with mixed emotions. We would be relocating in a larger city, high in the mountains. The climate change would be a relief. This unrelenting heat we had been enduring would become a memory, not an ongoing experience.

Ciudad Valles, though, had been our "baptism of fire"… our launching pad. We left good friends who had now become like brothers and sisters.

Our dear "best friends" and next-door neighbors had received the Lord when their son was diagnosed with cancer. As soon as we heard the diagnosis, we went to pray for him. And, of course, God healed him! (We were nearly as shocked as they were! We had not seen much of this up to this point working in the mountains) And, as one might expect, the entire family accepted the Lord after this. That young man is a Baptist minister today. PTL!

The kids and I had spent many an evening at our neighbor's house when Rory went to villages not deemed safe or easily accessible. These were areas best not to bring his family, it was agreed. Several times during our year there he was stopped on the road by men brandishing machetes and throwing rocks. But he went, and God always protected him.

I learned how to cook some wonderful Mexican dishes working alongside the grandma in that home. The kids spent hours playing games with the family. A favorite was "Loteria" a type of Bingo with Spanish words and pictures. That game was a winner with us as it gave us ongoing Spanish lessons.

That last day as we were enjoying our neighbors and their delicious food, I began to share with the ladies about a funny mistake I had made while speaking to the grandson of the family. I said it to get them all laughing; poking fun at myself, and then the dam broke! My darling neighbor began to tell story after story about the incredibly dumb things I had said during our time together. She had tears rolling down her cheeks as she recounted some things I had never realized I'd said! She talked about the names I called things and foodstuffs (always wrong) and the ridiculous words I had evidently made up in conversation! I'm sure I was beet red! I wish I could remember some specifics. I was so embarrassed, I probably put them out of my mind. The amazing thing is that during all our time there as neighbors, she had never even cracked a smile! Not once! Now, I often imagine how she must have burst into laughter the minute I went out her door. Our kitchen doors were maybe 6 feet apart; very close, but I never heard a peep. Wonderful people!

The parting was only mitigated by the knowledge that we would be back for visits from time to time. Hugs were exchanged and tears were shed while the kids made their own solemn good byes. "We'll see you again," we Christians say, "Here, there or in the air."

Lee Anne Worre Risk

Chapter 15

May, 1984
Zacatecas

This beautiful city was in existence long before the Spaniards arrived. An ancient Indian people inhabited this place before they were invaded and enslaved.

The city's streets were, and still are, narrow and cobbled. The old part of the city – El Centro – had been planned and constructed hundreds of years before automobiles existed. The streets had been fine for carts and burros. Now, only the fact that most motorized vehicles tended to be the so-called compacts and sub-compacts made the ancient streets traversable. Bicycles were everywhere and Mexican made VW's were beginning to be quite popular. The concept of "Buy now, Pay later" was not known yet. In past times, the average Mexican made do with travel by foot and bus till they could save enough for a car or truck. The Spanish had wasted little time in their quest to make Catholicism the religion of the land and erected, at the very center, the second oldest cathedral in all of Mexico. This grand edifice reared spires and steeples, the past looking down on the future; a rapidly modernizing commercial district.

La Bufa, a big loaf shaped bluff, loomed high on the other side of the city. Famous for being the site of a crucial battle between government forces and Pancho Villa's revolutionaries, La Bufa was an attraction for tourists. Not foreign tourists who had little interest in such things, but Mexicans, who often traveled far to visit this place where such momentous events had occurred. It was known also as a "high place," a place of religious significance.

One of the oldest silver mines in Mexico was dug deep into the hills around Zacatecas. It produced, and still does, the precious metal that was worked by skilled hands into every kind of adornment imaginable - hands that had been taught their skills generation after generation. Beautiful articles of agate and onyx set into silver rings and bracelets, necklaces, belts and hatbands were offered – one price for locals, another just a bit higher for tourists – highest of all for gringos – all over Zacatecas. Mexican capitalism at work.

Mexican construction is somewhat primitive by American standards, with rocks and concrete and cement blocks being the predominant building material. What some gringos call "poop bricks" a kind of mud adobe glued together with hay and manure, are also commonly used. Usually painted in bright primary colors, the houses make a kaleidoscope; a feast for the eyes, especially when the observer is on the upper side of a slope with the neighborhoods spread out below. There is seldom much imagination to the layout of a house. Rectangular would be the usual blueprint. That's why color is so important.

The entrance door to the houses was something intended to attract the attention of the visitor. Doors were made of pine or of a cheap variety of mahogany – Luan, it's called. The wood is cut thick so the doors are heavy. Then, often, the door is turned into a kind of flat sculpture with hand-carved shapes that make you stop for a moment and wonder what the door is trying to say. Those doors were well built. There is nothing like a good sturdy door to dissuade the opportunistic thievery that is so common in that culture.

Zacatecas felt like home almost immediately. Other missionaries working in the same general area were a huge help in getting us settled in. It took a while for us to get our bearings. We were directed to the best stores, the best mechanics, the best place for gas for the truck. When you show up as a new customer, every merchant you patronize becomes your friend. The kids found their way around our new neighborhood and soon had friends with which to run and play. As to be expected, being kids, they had far fewer barriers socially, and were quickly far more fluent in Spanish. Some of the slang was hard for us to decipher so we depended on our missionary friends to help us steer them away from the bad words.

The local Catholic Bishop was very upset by our presence in what he saw as his area to oversee and protect. He took out a full page ad in the newspaper warning people to stay away from us. Little printed signs began to appear in the windows of homes around us. The signs said "Protestants" were not welcome. It was hard not to feel sad and even a bit threatened by what seemed to be hostility.

But God is faithful and our batch of little blond children worked their way into people's homes by way of their quickly made Mexican friends. They played out in the street with those kids and soon we were accepted in nearly any home. In fact, we began to be invited to parties, weddings, birthdays and all kinds of get-togethers. Many of our neighbors became friends.

God gave us a good life and we saw fruit from the start.

Satan doesn't like that.

I believe our enemy is subject to the same things he tries to use to destroy us. One of his favorite tools is fear. If he can get us to be fearful, he can weaken us. Power, love, and a sound mind are God's provision for us, not a spirit of fear.

When any of us are being used of God, especially when we allow him to send us up to the front lines, Satan displays what we see as rage, but I think what spawns that rage is fear. I think Satan becomes terrified in the face of advances into his own territory by the soldiers of the Lord. We know he was and continues to be defeated by Christ's death and resurrection. He knows it too. The thought of the devil running scared helps explain the foolish and transparent attempts to sabotage God's work that our enemy so often displays. All he needs, oftentimes, is a little cooperation. And, oftentimes, he gets it.

Lee Anne Worre Risk

After a short while, I realized I would have to get some house help… for the floors, at least. If you missed more than a day of mopping, the fine sand from outside began to build up and soon it was like the Sahara desert on the first floor. It took a little longer to get tracked upstairs, but it made its way there as well. I had to spend hours with the kids each day as we were home-schooling them. Cooking was laborious too. Meals were made from scratch and it took some time to prepare them.

My neighbor told me that her girl helper had a sister who was looking for work. I invited her over. Her name was Maria and she was a darling… always smiling. We began to communicate as the days passed and I grew to love this sweet, quiet girl. She would listen politely when I tried to talk to her about Jesus, but demurred when asked to pray.

After Maria had been with us a few months, we learned we were to be assigned a family that we were to train for this work. As if we were experts. But we had a little experience and there were not many places that could offer this kind of education.

They were John and Debi Berger. Like us, they came right from language school. The two of them and their three kids became good friends immediately. It was comforting and enjoyable to have other like-minded people with which to fellowship. Around this same time, we had also developed a close relationship with some missionaries from the Agape Force. They had kids, but all but their oldest were a little too young to become pals with our kids. Their oldest, a terrific girl named Rebekah attached herself to our youngest, our Katy. They were together whenever possible with Rebekah often having a sleep-over at our house. God knew what Katy needed and Rebekah was just the ticket.

Debi soon recognized the need for help so we began to share Maria. It was with Debi that she finally bowed her head and gave her heart to the Lord. A great day! Our first convert here in Zacatecas!

We had begun Friday night movies at a little storefront a few blocks from our house. The idea was to create an attraction to draw people in and share Jesus with them. That's a proven way to get a new church planted. When we rented it, it was a mess. Some of those great kids from the Agape Force pitched in and helped make it presentable. Rory would drive all the way to Aguascalientes - a four hour trip - every week to get a Christian movie from a pastor who somehow managed to acquire them. Those movies were in the 16 millimeter format. They came in reels that were threaded into what was, even then, an archaic projector. Stories would be interrupted by malfunctions that sometimes required splicing broken film back together. Or the projector would slip a cog and the picture would vibrate and distort until the film was properly reset. (Older readers will remember that kind of thing.) I popped popcorn all day on Fridays till I filled a big black plastic garbage bag. Rory bought cases of little Cokes and we spread the word. Word of mouth did the trick. It was, of course, free, so that helped build the crowd.

We packed it out every week. After all the popcorn and soda had been passed around and when the movie was over, Rory would kind of recap the story they had seen and then give an "altar call" of sorts. Every time, every single one in the audience would raise their hands in response to the invitation. So exciting! The kids and I would walk around getting names, addresses and phone numbers, if they had a phone, that is. We wanted to follow up and begin to nurture them in their walk. When we went to find them over the next day or so, we found out the information we had been given was made up. They all provided false names and addresses. They were trying to spare our feelings. They had not talked among themselves and planned to deceive us, they just didn't want to embarrass us or make us feel bad. In Mexico, the culture gives people the idea that it's not really a lie if what you are trying to do is help people not feel bad. The Mexicans understand what's going on, but we Americans struggle with it; especially the Christians, I suppose. Ah, how we live and, hopefully, learn. Thinking about it afterwards and even laughing a little, we were reminded of the sometimes subtle power of the Gospel. Does God's word ever return void? Of course not. As time passed we saw evidence of lives touched and souls saved. We planted... and watered.

We started Sunday morning services at around this same time. At first, it was just us. Just our family. Then a young man from Tijuana showed up. He told us he had been saved there but now had come south to find work. Javier was his name. Bless his heart. He would faithfully attend church with us every Sunday. We treated him as if he were a crowd. We would start with Praise and Worship. I had a little Casio keyboard and I would bang out the choruses with the family and Javier lustily singing along. The kids would take the offering, (Gotta have an offering) and would participate with a peso or two we had given them to get them in the habit. Then Rory would deliver a sermon for which he had spent hours preparing. That old joke about the evangelist who came to a rural area and only one old farmer showed up comes to mind. The evangelist preached his heart out and when he was done and the old fellow was leaving, asked him what he thought of the sermon. "Well," the farmer replied, "If I go out to feed the herd with a wagon full of feed and only one cow shows up, I don't usually give him the whole load." Rory was the one who remembered the joke, but never was criticized in that way, and the sermon was as much for him, he said, as it was for whoever was within hearing.

Maria had been helping at the house for some time and when she got saved, she began to attend church services, too. She brought her sister, and her sister gave her life to Jesus. She brought her mother and she found the Lord, as well. The Holy Spirit was on the move. One day Maria came to us with the news that she had a boyfriend and wanted to get married. Rory asked her to bring him over to meet us and she smilingly complied. When she showed up with Chuy (a nickname for Jesus), we were appalled. He was as thin as a rail - skin and bones, as they say. He was clearly addicted to some kind of strong drugs. We sat down and began to talk. Maria loved him and so did the Lord. His life was going in a bad direction and as we talked, the Holy Spirit began to work on his heart. When Chuy heard that God loved him and Jesus died for his sins, he was overwhelmed. Rory introduced him to Jesus and Chuy joyfully accepted Him as Savior and Lord. Chuy got saved! We had a friend who worked in Uruapan who called those converts whose lives were dramatically changed "Good saved". Chuy got "Good saved!"

Chuy brought his brother, his sister, his mother and some cousins. They all began to be followers of Jesus.

As can be expected, some of these new believers got pretty vocal and evangelical with their friends and families. That will happen in almost any culture. Some became ostracized from their former circle because of their zealous denunciation of their families' traditional religion. As new Christians, their own eyes were opened to the deception religion had endorsed. They wanted their families and friends to have their eyes opened as well. When cut off from their past circle, they naturally gravitated to us. We tried to teach them ways to show the love of the Lord without being harshly offensive. We showed them that a heart change is a powerful witness. As I write this, I am reminded of what the Bible says. The Gospel can be an offense. As we live it out, it should either attract or repel. We are often far too willing to try to please everybody. I guess that's where wisdom comes in.

Our little work grew. It got to where we had as many as one hundred people in a service. It had to be Easter to get to that number, but we had a body of believers. We had enough strong Christians to set up cell groups in five different areas in the twin cities of Zacatecas and Guadalupe. The members of each cell traveled by bus or even on foot to attend every time those groups met. It got to the point where there was something going on every night of the week. That kind of schedule began to be a little strenuous on our family so we started taking an occasional Monday off. Some were coming from the states to visit in those days and, of course, we felt we needed to entertain them. We never felt like we needed a break from that obligation. If no visitors were there to see us and our local folks were not pressing, we would leave town for the day and go to Aguascalientes or San Luis Potosi and do things with the kids. We found things to do that we never had a chance to do in Zacatecas. Things like bowling or even just walking through an air conditioned mall.

In those days, there were few homes with "laundry rooms." My washing machine was twenty five years old. It had done the wash for several missionary families before I inherited it. We had it hooked up in a corner of our uncovered patio. If it rained, the wash waited. That washing machine had seen better days, but it washed clothes and kept going. When you hear the phrase, "a mover and a shaker" you think of some energetic businessman. That phrase also fit this machine. There was no longer anything automatic about how it worked. I had to run out to the patio and advance the cycles to finish a load of clothes. I was out there one glorious spring day doing what had to be done. The washer tried to dance all over the patio during the spin cycle, so I had to lean over and put as much of my weight on it as I could in order to hold it down. Good thing I was no skinny little thing. For as long as it took to finish the cycle, I would hold on and spend the time looking out over the mountain. I would thank the Lord for the wonderful life He had given us. I loved our life! I couldn't imagine how it could be any better.

Lee Anne Worre Risk

Chapter 17

Summer 1986
Monday morning

A pretty day. Sunday had gone well. Some new visitors and a good sermon. Still feeling the glow, I began to prepare breakfast. Eggs and tortillas and this day, some spicy Chorizo sausage. Fresh coffee brewed and percolated, adding its rich aroma to the smells of the food being cooked. A bird perched on a twiggy limb outside the kitchen window and began to offer the best justification for its existence; singing for all it was worth. Traffic buzzed and chuckled along on the street below, making a sound that had become silence to us. The water truck pulled up close and the man fed the hose from his truck to the cistern braced awkwardly on the roof. Those water tanks adorned every roof in the city, marring the view from where, on the side of a hill above and overlooking the city at large, our house was situated. If the water main was broken and the water truck was ever delayed, there would be no dishes washed or, for sure, no showers taken and no toilets flushed. That water cost money, so the 4 or 5 gallons it took to flush the toilet made us all infrequent flushers. The slogan we lived by? "If it's yellow, let it mellow. If it's brown, flush it down."

I was picking up after the kids when a young woman came to our door. She was a tiny little thing and had a baby peeking out from her arms.

"Please, senora. Is there some work I can do for you? I am in need of employment. I need to buy food for my children."

"I'm sorry, senora," I said. "We can't use anyone right now, but let me get you some food to take with you." I went after some fruit and gave it to her. I smiled at the baby and said good bye.

She was persistent, returning every day or so to make her petition again. In the meantime, our little Maria had fallen in love and gotten married; leaving our employ. One day I was faced with more busyness than usual but saw her coming and opened the door before she knocked.

"Have you used an electric iron before?"

"Si, senora. See my dress? I can iron for you."

And so our lives with Marta began.

I have thought since about her persistence. Was there no other work at all? It was almost as if she had been sent or had picked us out and had persevered until she got her way.

She was pleasant and quiet. We had coffee and talked from time to time. Almost always, she had the baby with her. We all fussed over the tiny girl. She didn't cry a lot and would survey the scene before her with solemn eyes.

We talked about the Lord when we had a chance. Christians everywhere and anywhere should always be ready to "give an account."

Marta carried an air of melancholy, not smiling often.

"My husband has become a drunkard," she explained one day. "He was not so bad when we were first married. Now he is drunk every day and beats me. If I did not earn money, we would be hungry." She looked down and away. "My children are little and sometimes he beats them too."

My heart broke. "Oh, honey. I've been telling you how much Jesus loves you. He is one who will watch over you. He loves your husband, too," I added. She nodded, but looked skeptical.

Marta began to come to church and one day raised her hand when the invitation was given. I was not there that day, but had every confidence that our ladies knew how to pray with someone and introduce them to Jesus.

In those days, Marta and I were fast friends. She loved to have her hair tended to and as soon as the curls subsided would be after me for another permanent.

"We should go and visit Marta's family," I suggested one day.

"Sure," Rory said. "Let's invite ourselves over. Would tomorrow night work?"

That was kind of a "Mexican" thing to do – go to people's houses and visit. Not an odd thing to do, at all. When we told Marta we wanted to drop in at her house, she seemed happy, but a little nervous.

"I will tell my husband... or maybe not tell him," she said. "If he knows you are coming, he might not stay home."

He was home. It was a bit of an honor, perhaps, to have these Americans come to his house. Also, it would have been discourteous to avoid our visit.

Marta invited us in and fluttered around the room that served as kitchen/living room/dining area. The house was tiny. Three rooms in all. It was located inside the city, so had rudimentary plumbing and electricity. In size, it reminded me some of our little railroad car when I was growing up. In appearance, it was very different. Walls of rough plaster painted white. Ceiling once white, but now darkened to a yellow brown from cooking fumes and tobacco smoke. A few pictures hung haphazardly here and there and a board with a row of coat hooks was screwed into the wall near the door. The floor in the main room was the common brown tile, several of those with broken corners and vacant spaces where tiles had come loose and been lost. The bedroom floors were beaten down dirt. A hand-made counter sat next to a battered and stained wall-hung sink. As in nearly every home in Mexico, a picture of the Virgin Mary hung on the wall over the sink alongside of a picture of a pope from three popes ago. Curtains made of cheap cotton adorned the windows. They were clean and brightened up the room.

"Coffee?" Marta asked timidly. It was the commonly used instant coffee and we sat around the little table and sipped while we visited. We could hear the children in the bedroom, and once in a while, one of them would open the door and peek at us. Jose was a little inebriated, but was willing to talk. We discussed the subjects people anywhere in the world might bring up. The weather; not much to say there. Pretty predictable in Zacatecas. Maybe rain. Maybe not. Maybe chilly. Maybe not. Got off that subject pretty quickly and on to politics. Back then all Mexicans revered their president, mayor, etc. We did not disabuse them of that notion. Family; spent some time hearing about relatives, far and near and, in case the children were listening, some discussion of the way the schools were working and a little mention (not too much) of how well they were doing. Parents the world over seem to feel it's not a good idea to let your kids get the idea that you are overly proud of them. Having already broached talk regarding politics, we tried to side-step into the other no-no; religion. Since they were well aware that we were in Mexico as missionaries, it really was not that awkward to bring up. When we did, it was done gently but with confidence. We shared how a relationship with the Lord Jesus Christ could not only change lives, but being born again could insure a home in heaven. Marta sat to one side, watching closely to see how Jose would react. She held herself still, only her eyes moving as one spoke and another. Always checking for a reaction in her husband. Seemingly, not seeing in her husband what she wanted to see.

As we headed for home, we talked about how we would have loved to have been a mouse in the corner after we left. Just to know what they said to each other would have been fascinating.

We visited a few more times. Each visit seemed to bring Jose closer to a decision. It was a great day when Rory knelt with him and led him to the Lord.

Chapter 18

April 1987

Rory went on being himself. He spread gentle humor along with a dose of Jesus wherever he went. He was just a nice person. He was able to make anyone feel special – make them feel singled out and cared about. And he treated Marta in that same way. She began to believe that Rory truly felt something special about her. It seemed that she was developing a crush on him. Before long, her infatuation became very apparent. She lit up whenever he talked to her or even glanced in her direction. Her eyes tracked him whenever he was in the room. She began to actually follow him as he moved about the house. Her adulation was so over-the-top it was kind of comical. Our kids mocked her attitude and the way she followed him around. They were making fun, but not to her face.

In August, we made a trip to Minnesota to visit some of our supporting churches. One prominent church was Calvary Temple, pastored by Rory's friend, Gordon Peterson. Rory preached that Sunday and when the sermon was over, Gordy asked the elders of the church to come up, gather around us and pray over us. We always saw this kind of attention as very important; a profoundly spiritual event. When they had prayed, one of the elders; a highly respected member of the elder board there at Calvary, took my arm and pulled me aside to speak softly in my ear. "The Lord is telling me that Satan has desired to sift you like wheat…but God says you will not be moved. He says you will stand firm." I looked up at him and nodded, thinking that it was somewhat odd, but certainly scriptural. At that point, the only thing I could think of that could relate was that my youngest was about to become a teenager. Three teenagers at one time can be a nightmare, I had been told. Good sifting material, I thought. The plans Satan had for me – the things that actually faced me would make that a trivial thought indeed. That elder's prophetic word for me lay buried in my consciousness for a long time; even during the sifting itself.

Months passed during which Marta's attachment to my husband appeared to grow. I said nothing to him for all that time, but it became too obvious for me to ignore. When I finally mentioned her behavior to Rory, he poo-pooed my concern.

"She's married, Lee Anne," he said. "She has four little kids."

"I know, Rory," I said. "That makes it even more of a potential problem."

"She's a nice girl," he said. "I'll be careful how I act around her."

Marta's husband quit drinking and began to grow in his walk with the Lord. Marta seemed to take no notice of the change in him. Jose was now a hard-working fellow and had a strong love for his family. Marta was looking elsewhere - seemingly not impressed with the change.

Jose came to me one day that fall; a day when Marta was not working.

"Senora," he said, wringing his hat in his hands, "May I talk with you for a minute?"

"Of course," I said. "Come in and sit."

"It is very difficult for me to talk to you this way," he said. "I have much to be thankful for and you and your family have been a large part of that. I have Jesus in my heart. He is my Lord and Savior. I have heaven for my home. All this is very good."

I nodded and saw his face twist in frustration.

"It is my wife, Marta," he went on. "She is changed. She seems discontented with me. She no longer sleeps with me." His eyes welled up. "Before I gave my heart to Jesus, I was not a good husband. I would get drunk and, I'm ashamed to say, I would hit her ... my own little Marta. But I am different now, praise to the Lord. I love her and I am working to provide for her and my children. I never hit her anymore and, by God's grace, I will never hit her again. In spite of these things, she says she doesn't love me at all now." Tears rolled down his cheeks. "I know it cannot be your fault, and I only come to you because I am confused and don't know what to do." I offered him a tissue and he wiped his nose.

"She talks of nothing but your husband. She looks at me with disdain and tells me of the wonderful things he does. She says to me that he has a special love for her and he will take far better care of her than I ever could. She says his name all the time. She says he is a better man than me. I am losing her." He looked up at me, pleading in his eyes. "Could it be true? Does he love her in that way? Marta says that you don't appreciate him like she does. Can anything be done to fix this? I feel like I'm getting crazy from this!"

"What you are saying concerns me greatly," I said. "This is wrong and I'm sure Marta will come to her senses. I will talk to my husband. He will agree that she should not be acting and feeling this way. Believe me," I said confidently, "this will not continue. We love you - you and your family. You, Jose, are our brother in Christ. We will be praying for the Holy Spirit to make everything clear to Marta. She is His child, as well."

He left at around 1:00 and I began to finish putting our lunch together. I started to pray. "God, you know all about this situation and I am at a loss as to what to do. Please work on her heart and help me to help her?" I was concerned, but not alarmed.

There are a lot of things that must be done differently at higher altitudes. Cooking took quite a bit more time than when at sea level. Water boiled at a much lower temperature, for example. Baking was even touchier. If I had no seasoned native nearby from which to get advice, I would have to experiment. Take it out of the oven, stick a fork in it and put it back in. Baked some pretty raw stuff till I got it all figured out.

I had previously cleaned and sorted the beans for that day. We would be having the "Flor de Mayo" kind. That was one of our favorites of the many kinds that are available in this area of Mexico. That morning I had put them in water and started them cooking while I chopped up some typically tough beef (cows in Mexico eat cactus) to make a "guiso"…kind of a meat vegetable mixture with chiles and lots of garlic and onion. It had a very thin gravy, too. It was always served with beans and rice and the inexpensive and easy to get corn tortillas. We had a tortilleria right up the block. Corn meal mixed into a dough, flattened and baked fresh. Rory John would go and be back in under five minutes if the line was not too long.

Rice prep was something I had learned from the church ladies. I washed the rice first and then let it drain while I started heating up corn oil in the frying pan. When the oil was hot enough, I dumped the rice in and started to fry it. I like it best when the rice fries to an almost pink color. Then I added what I had already prepared in the blender; tomatoes, onions, salt and sometimes some spices. I added water; enough to finish cooking the rice and have it turn out. I would often fry up nopales, too. Nopales is a tender cactus leaf that is first chopped and boiled and then fried with a little bacon, oregano, tomatoes and onions. At least that is how our family liked it best! I continued to pray as I cooked until Rory came home from the bank.

Rory came into the kitchen and sat down at the table. I expected him to make some appreciative comment about the good smell of the food. Uncharacteristically, he said nothing. I had been hoping for a good opening to bring up Jose's visit.

"Jose came today," I said tentatively.

"What did he want?"

"He was pretty upset."

"What's his problem," he said, his tone belligerent. "Asking for money?"

"Why would you say that?" I said. "He has never done that."

"What, then?"

"He came about Marta. He thinks their marriage is failing. I know you don't think it's that much of an issue, but she has a crush – more than a crush, I think – on you."

Rory sat there, rigid and unresponsive.

I went on. "He feels he can't compete with you. He's not saying right out that he's blaming you, but I can tell he's holding you responsible, at least in part."

"How can he be serious? Lee Anne, how can *you* be serious? What would you suggest I do? I should be unfriendly to this poor little woman? What kind of ministry will we have if we don't show care and concern for these people and their hurts? Marta is part of our church family! Marta is our sister in the Lord, Lee Anne."

I was taken aback. "Maybe I'm off base here, Rory. You're my husband and I trust you, but it seems pretty clear that something has to change. I don't know exactly what or who or how it might happen, but this is becoming more and more of a problem. Lately she has adopted an attitude with me. I don't know exactly how to describe it, but it is as if she believes she has a place with you that puts me behind her; makes her superior to me. I don't know where this is coming from, but it's not healthy."

"This is stupid," he said. "I'll talk to her and I'll talk to him. I'll take care of it."

"And isn't Jose part of our church family, too?" I said, softly.

Nothing changed in our house. After that it was weeks later that Jose came back to me telling me that the only change in his relationship with his wife was that it was getting worse.

Our fellow missionary, Robert, had something to say to me about the way things looked with Marta and Rory and her presence in our house. He must have made similar comments to Rory as well. He was close to Rory and sensed real danger in the situation. I had not felt very much concern until Jose came back with that second bleak report. At that point, I began to believe there was something to Robert's warnings. I brought it up to Rory again after that second visit. I waited till the kids were out playing.

"Rory," I began, "you're my husband. I look to you as the head of our family. I want to do what you say." I stopped, feeling very out of place and still unsure of how to talk to him. We rarely had any kind of real disagreement about anything, but I could sense his obstinacy on this subject.

I just blurted it out. "With everything that has been happening; her husband, this attachment for you, her attitude, and the things others are noticing, I'm sorry, but I don't feel comfortable with her here in our home."

"So you want to kick her out, then. What a great testimony that would be," he sneered.

"Why do you want to say it that way," I said. "Letting her go isn't 'kicking her out'."

"It amounts to the same thing," he said. "You just want to make it sound nicer"

"Keeping her on will only make the problem worse, in my opinion. And, Rory, please believe me when I say that I want what the Lord wants in this. I have prayed long and hard for God's will to be clear in this thing. If things continue the way they are, our whole ministry here could be damaged or ruined."

I hadn't wanted to come right out and say it, but what I felt was real danger. This woman could start rumors and spread lies that could tear our testimony to shreds.

"That's your opinion," he said, almost shouting. "I guess you feel I'm not entitled to mine."

"Don't say that, Rory. You know I always look to you for any decision. Do you think I hate her? I don't, but we need to be wise. We both know that our ministry is under constant attack by the Devil. We need to use wisdom."

I was pleading. This was such a painful discussion. Our marriage was idyllic in my thinking. We were in sync on everything that mattered. Our kids never saw us arguing or fighting. My heart was pounding. Rory was red-faced and furious. All I could think was, "Lord, help us!"

"This is stupid," he said. "She needs this job. Her husband isn't a good enough provider."

"Maybe not, but there must be other places she can work. We can even help her find something. The way he talks, their marriage is in serious trouble. Working here seems to be making things worse. I've been thinking I might try to counsel her in how to relate to her husband. God hates divorce and it seems they are headed in that direction. What a tragedy that would be."

"Wonderful idea. You - her counselor," he sneered. "As if she could receive from you. You're jealous, Lee Anne. I see it now.

Jealous of a poor little woman who's only trying to take good care of her kids and be a blessing to us."

I stood there with my mouth hanging open. I was flabbergasted. This was so preposterous I almost laughed. Before I could say anything, he stood and put his coffee down. "Lee Anne," he said, "if you let Marta go, it will be you that does it. I'll say this as plainly as I can. I think it's a bad idea – not wisdom at all. I think it will be wrong. I am not in agreement with you. Do you understand me?" With that, he stormed out of the room and a moment later, I heard the door slam as he left the house. With that statement, Rory delivered a crushing blow. And he knew exactly how it would make me feel. In a Christian marriage, the wife needs to honor her husband as the head. We taught marriage seminars together and always emphasized the importance of a united front as a testimony and to create the kind of strength every marriage needs. His refusal to see the problem and danger in this situation made me feel guilty and sad. This was so confusing. As I am writing this, I still wonder if my adamant insistence in letting Marta go in the face of Rory's opposition was right. I have searched my heart, though, and I know my motive was love. Love for Rory – love for Marta and her family and a desire for our ministry to go forward.

The next day, I called Marta into the kitchen and, seated in the same chairs we had occupied in many times of friendly fellowship, got ready to tell her I was letting her go. She could tell from my demeanor that this was not going to be a friendly chat. She was sullen. I was nervous.

"Marta, it's hard for me to do this, but I have to let you go." My voice trembled as I spoke.

She looked at me with narrowed eyes. "Why, senora? Am I not doing my work well?" I know she was fully aware of my reasons.

"It's not that, Marta. I just feel its best – for both of our families."

"My husband has come here and made trouble," she said.

"Not trouble, Marta. Your husband loves you and is only trying to do what he can to please you," I said.

"I am not pleased. He is worthless to me," she said stiffly. She got up from the table and turned to leave. "I think you will be sorry you did this, senora," she said and abruptly left the house.

I prayed that God would help her understand. That next Sunday, her husband came to church, but Marta did not.

We still needed a little help around the house and found a lady from church that worked out fine. We were all able to relax a little bit with having Marta in the house no longer an issue. All except Rory. Rory wasn't relaxed. He didn't talk about it or throw it in my face, but he changed.

"Mom, why is dad being such a jerk all the time?" my son, Rory John asked one day.

I was surprised at his question. He always acted like his father could do no wrong. Of course, he was just barely a teen-ager. "What a way to talk," I said. "He's your father and deserves your respect."

But what he was seeing was a man who was surly and cold, when he had always been cheerful and warm. A man who had begun to exhibit strange behavior. The phone would ring and Rory would leap to answer it. Once in a while, he would carry on a brief conversation with the caller. When asked, it was always just "someone from church." His attitude didn't encourage further questioning. If he had been out, the first thing he would say when he returned was, "Were there any phone calls?" When there had been, we would tell him how many there were, but also that sometimes no one answered when we picked up. He would get agitated. "How many times did it ring on those calls?" It seemed like he was accusing us of doing something wrong, but we couldn't figure out what was bothering him.

He had long had a habit of going for walks every morning to think and pray. Those walks got longer and longer – a change in his behavior that nagged at me when I thought about it. Our life was undergoing a steady slide into distrust and depression. God, help us.

Chapter 19

March 1988

We found out a couple of years later that Marta had done something that had given her an odd kind of confidence about her relationship with Rory. That arrogant attitude she had begun to take with me was a result of that incident. Marta had set her sights on Rory and in order to get what she wanted, she had gone to a local witch doctor. Marta's brother was the one that told us about it. He said she had given that old shaman "a lot of money" to put a spell on Rory and a curse on me. Ironically, the money she used to pay him was money she had gotten from Rory, himself. In order to get it from him, she had told him she needed it to get a bed and mattress. That money had come from people who supported our work and intended it to be used to spread the Gospel. How diabolical that it would be spent in such a way. Marta believed in the witch's power and began to act on that belief. She began to take her place - the place that had once been mine - in his life at once. At that point, whether he realized it fully or not, Rory was beginning to cooperate with the spell cast on him. He was being beguiled and

Satan was moving in. I'm sure Marta fully expected that I would be taken out of the picture in one way or another before too long. She was not far wrong.

We always talked after going to bed – sometimes long into the night. Those conversations were comfortable and intimate. Our best time for real communication.

Then, the most terrible night of my life. On that night, we lay in silence for a while and then Rory began to talk. At first, I thought he was having a nightmare and talking in his sleep. Then I thought I might be dreaming. His teeth were clenched and he spewed terrible things about what a waste of a person I was; how unattractive and useless I was to him. What was coming out of his mouth was so vile, so determinably hurtful, so uncharacteristically hate-filled that I lay there stunned and speechless. In the midst of this flood of invective, he leaned over to put his face in mine. His expression was so enraged that he was almost unrecognizable. Like someone possessed.

I couldn't stand it. I was frantically trying to find some way to agree with him. Surely, I thought. I must be the wrong-doer. But his accusations were so outlandish that I couldn't find a way to make sense of them. Something broke in me. What reason could there be to go forward? *He doesn't love me. He has come to hate me.* What he was saying was so terrible, I couldn't feel any hope for his feelings to change and for him to once again become the man I knew. If this was how things were going to be, I had no heart, no reason to continue. In a kind of black despair, I got out of bed, picked up my purse and went into the bathroom. Something was urging me to do the best thing for everybody.

For a diabetic, suicide is simple. Enough insulin and you go into a coma and then you die. Normally, I would not take the time to find my purse just to go to the bathroom during the night. Rory watched me take it and knew it was not something I would typically do. I took it because the things I would need to end my life were among its contents. I did not feel the comforting presence of the Lord. I felt alone and unloved. God was there, of course, and He was in control, but I had no sense of Him being there with me.

I began to prepare to inject the overdose of insulin. Then, God came into my consciousness and intervened. My mind cleared and I was able to step back and see things from His perspective. Who was I to think I could take my own life? Such arrogance. Suicide is the ultimate demonstration of selfishness and distrust. It says that God is somehow helpless and can only stand to one side and watch your pain with sympathetic eyes. I was suddenly reminded of my children. The thought of how my death would affect them brought me back to reality. I would be gone, and this suddenly crazy man would be their only parent.

Still desperately distraught, and wishing all this pain to end; wanting this all to be over and not having to face this inconceivable horror, I, none the less, put the syringe back in my purse.

Two terrible thoughts spun through my mind. One – I had come to the very brink of suicide. Two – It seemed certain that Rory had known I might have intended it when I took my purse, but had been unwilling to do anything to stop me.

I came back to bed. Rory was laying there, a remorseful look on his face.

"LeeAnne, I said some of the stupidest things. I didn't mean any of them. Please forgive me."

I didn't say anything, just got back into bed. Lying next to him, I kept thinking, *he wanted me to do it*. Was he hoping I would? He moved over to put his arms around me. He held me for a while and kept whispering sweet loving words. The thoughts of him not loving me and wanting me gone drifted away. I went to sleep comforted. I woke up hopeful. Rory was up before I was. He stood, rigid, by the kitchen counter. One look at his face told me he was anything but pleased to see me. When I saw his attitude, how angry he was, seemingly because I was still alive, despair returned.

You might be able to understand how that night's events began to fade in my mind. Painful things have a way of lessening with time. We have this mechanism – God given, I believe, that gives us the capacity to take pain and bury it beneath the surface of our memories. Every woman who has experienced child-birth can testify to this phenomenon. That capacity helps us stay sane. It can also have a negative effect by keeping us from absorbing the full value of our experience. We went to talk to some missionary friends that morning to try to get some counsel. It was not an encouraging visit. After that conversation, I realized that things might not get better; that our marriage was in serious trouble. I began to fixate on the "me and my house" scripture and prayed for faith to believe it. In just a day or so, Rory and I were talking and acting almost as if nothing had happened and everything was just fine. However, something fundamental had changed for us. When you have been treated in this kind of way, it's as if you have been lied to. You even kind of wish you didn't know how that person feels because now you have to distrust and verify everything they say or do. When a relationship gets to that point, you become emotionally exhausted.

Rory's habit had always been to get up early and go out and walk, think, and pray. This continued to be his daily routine all during this traumatic time. As I said, the walks were getting longer now. Marta was gone and, I assumed, out of our lives. I knew Rory cared about her and wanted things to go well for her. I tried to trust that his concern was Godly.

A friend stopped by one day and casually mentioned that she had seen Rory talking with Marta behind the school. I made excuses to the friend. "He must have run into her and stopped to say hello," I said. "Just being kind to her," I said, as much to myself as to my friend.

Life was depressing. Our home was an uncomfortable place in which to be. Days passed and I performed the wifely role, but felt threatened and afraid and would have little attacks of sheer panic. Church felt sort of contrived. God was still God, and His work kept going forward, but seemingly, without much of our involvement.

At that point, I entered what would be the bleakest period of my life up to that time. If I had known what lay ahead, that knowledge might have pushed me over the edge.

Rory and I were mostly civil, but any attempts by me to go beyond the impersonal in our conversations were met with silence and/or a look that showed cold animosity. The kids were very aware that something was wrong, but didn't comment much. I just mentioned that we were going through something and that I would explain it to them some time later.

After Jesus was baptized by John, The Holy Spirit led Him out into the wilderness, away from everyone, and the scripture says; "left Him there." It seems to suggest that God was nowhere around, yet we know that one of the attributes that sets Him apart from all else is His omnipresence. I think Jesus was made to feel alone; to lose His awareness of His Father's presence. The lesson for us is when we find ourselves in that place where the heavens are like brass, we can still make the decision to trust Him. No matter how abandoned and alone we might feel, our past experience and our knowledge of His imperishable word gives us all we need to withstand the temptation to give up. His oversight and protection are a constant, whether we feel it or not. Faith, faith that comes by hearing, is the tool to use, and God supplies it.

I began to go out at night after the kids were in bed and asleep. There was a kind of gazebo in the middle of the fairgrounds not far away. I would usually gravitate to that place. Late at night, there was little chance of anyone else being out and about. It was often very dark, especially when it was a cloudy night with no stars or moon visible. You can hide in the dark. Sometimes you want to hide; to be unseen. I knew God could see me, but was tormented by the idea that He was displeased with me. On many nights, I would just sit there in the square and cry and pray, sometimes for hours. I asked God over and over what I might have done or failed to do to provoke this behavior in my life-partner. I begged Him to "search me and know my thoughts" but was given no clear answer. I still have questions about why He couldn't give me some way to see past the terrible trouble in the midst of which I found myself. All I can think of now was how my Savior was betrayed by someone close to him. What was happening to me felt like the ultimate betrayal. When I would finally make my way back to our house and get into bed next to my husband, what sleep I got was troubled and beset by terrible dreams.

How could this happen? I must have rehearsed every possible scenario a hundred times since all this happened.

This painful and stressful set of circumstances went on day after day. My heart was breaking and I felt helpless to do anything to make things right.

Rory had a friend from the states that was going to be staying fairly close to us for a week or so. He called Rory and asked if they would be able to get together in Monterey. Rory seemed glad to hear from him and drove up to Monterey to spend a couple of days just being together. His friend had gone into the ministry as well, so they would have a lot to talk about. I was encouraged by the way Rory acted as he left. When he came back, he slipped back into what he was before. That is, he was still sullen and uncommunicative. It's hard for me to say I lost hope, but I did feel pretty hopeless.

The winter, such as it is in Zacatecas, was over. Our wedding anniversary was coming up in a few weeks. I had a medical issue that had been a long standing problem. We made plans to go to the border together. I would then go on to Minnesota for minor surgery. The trip was already planned. We left as planned. That was before the world, as I knew it, came to an abrupt end.

Chapter 20

The recovery
June 1988

My recovery went in fits and starts. The hospital stay was long. My back was so bad they ended up fitting me with a full-body cast made of fiberglass. I had been supine for so long that being raised to a vertical position made me pass out. Physical therapy was excruciating, but there seemed to be some hope on the doctor's part that I would, after a time become mobile, at least to some degree.

Anissa, my oldest, had traveled with me to Minnesota, but went back to Mexico soon after I was hospitalized. I knew that was the best thing at the time. My son, Rory and youngest daughter, Katy were home alone. Neighbors were close by, of course but the kids were barely into their teens.

Not just because of the laws, but more because of the corrupt culture in Mexico, Rory had been detained by the authorities for two days. They really wanted the truck. Robert, our missionary friend went back to see to the kids.

Anissa took the bus from the border to Zacatecas. When she got home, her little sister told her about a strange phone conversation she had overheard. She put it out of her mind, but a few days later while she was out walking with a friend, she saw her father with Marta in an area known to be where lovers liked to go. Katy's report of the strange phone call came back to her. She knew what she was seeing was not right.

A little while later, Robert took his wife to a women's clinic in San Luis Potosi. Rory had been released and gone back to the kids a week or so prior, but while they were at the clinic, Robert saw Rory and Marta was with him. Evidently, Marta was seeing the doctors there as well. Marta already had a history of using various medical and physical problems as ploys to keep Rory near her and sympathetic. There had been some bogus attempts at suicide over the previous months. Now, she was claiming to have cancer. Rory had brought her to the clinic for diagnosis and treatment.

For some time, Robert had his suspicions about Marta and Rory's relationship. As I have related, Rory's behavior had become so erratic, it was hard for people not to wonder. He decided to follow them to where they were staying. It was a small cabin; one of a little group built to house patients and their families while they were being treated. Robert quickly determined that it was a simple, one-room affair – hardly appropriate for anyone other than a married couple. He waited a bit, and when Rory emerged, Robert confronted him. When he did, Rory ran away from him. Robert ran after him, but Rory literally took to the rooftops and got away. Robert went home in anger and disgust.

I was in no condition to be informed about this craziness and was kept unaware.

Lee Anne Worre Risk

In Minnesota, I was going through hell on earth with pain – both emotional and physical. Time passed, but oh, so slowly. "Time flies when you're having fun," they say, but it sure does crawl when you're suffering.

After about a month, Rory got the kids loaded up in the truck and headed north to Minneapolis. As they neared Minneapolis and on their last stop for food, he brought them into a restaurant and tried to tell them what was going on.

"Your mom's hurt bad," he told them. "You kids are going to have to pull together. She's going to need your help. All the help you can give her." They listened, staring at him. There was something wrong with what he was saying. It sank in later that he was telling them that he wasn't going to be there. It was them who would be responsible. At that time, though, they assured him they would be good.

Rory left them for a few minutes to go to the restroom. While he was gone, Anissa, frustrated and heartsick, sternly cautioned the other two; "When we get to mom, don't tell her about how dad talked. It isn't good and she is too sick to have to hear it."

Rory brought them in to see me. Having them there was probably the best therapy I could ask for. Then he got them situated with relatives and then immediately headed back to Mexico. Everyone advised him to stay, but he insisted that he had to go.

"I can't stay," he said. "I know I should, but what help am I here? I know I am needed in Zacatecas. I have to get back down there."

My son came over to spend some time with me one day and the conversation came around to his dad. I was talking calmly about how I was going to get better and how nice it was going to be to be back in Zacatecas. Rory John sat there listening. He knew the truth, but he never said a word.

Chapter 22

July 1988

After a couple months in the hospital, suddenly a lot happened, and it all happened pretty fast. Unbeknownst to me, Rory took Marta and her children and fled Zacatecas. First stop, Baja. Kind of strategic, being close to California. The Tijuana border crossing then allowed fairly easy access to the US. The Mexicans would walk across and Rory, being a US citizen could drive through and pick them up on the other side.

At this point, I was getting regular rehab therapy from the hospital staff and gals from church. I needed this help because the hospital would not give me a release until I could, at least, take sixteen steps in the walker and could show I was able to get in and out of a car. By the time Rory started moving Marta and her kids around, I was out of the hospital and staying in the home of very dear friends, Cal and Eloise Hedlund. I remember that Linda Strom came faithfully to give me massages, help me stretch and practice in the walker. Those women were such a blessing. We worked and practiced and one great day, they took me outside. The warm sun and fresh air felt so wonderful. And the greenest green I could ever remember crowned the trees and carpeted the lawns. I promised myself I would try to never take these things for granted. God's world is wonderful.

Rory called while I was there, but kept the conversation clear of any mention of Marta until the last week I was there. Katy happened to be "mom-sitting". The phone rang and I picked it up.

"Hello?"

"LeeAnne, we have to do something about the church in Zacatecas," my husband shouted. He seemed almost hysterical and sounded out of control.

"Why? What's the matter?" I asked, feeling my stomach tighten in alarm at his tone.

"I had to leave there," he cried. "Someone needs to be there to take care of our people!"

"You left? Why did you leave?"

"Please," he said. "Call and get someone down there. Someone we can trust. I can't make foreign phone calls where I am."

"Where are you? What in the world is going on?" My heart was beating like a trip hammer. It didn't sink in then that he was calling from somewhere in the states.

"Lee Anne, I had to take Marta and her kids and run. Her husband is making violent threats. I'm trying to protect them!"

"Rory, this is bad," I said. "This is a bad idea."

He ignored me. "We've taken a bus to Baja. We think he may have talked to the police. We had to get away!"

"No, Rory. Don't do this. Send her back. Send her and her kids back."

"This is hard, Lee Anne. I feel responsible. They need help. I'm just trying to help them."

I was crying almost uncontrollably now and tried to talk through my tears.

"Think, Rory. You know this is wrong. No good can come of it."

He paused and calmed down a bit. "Ok, Lee Anne. That's what I'll do. I'll send them back."

"Good," I said. "It's the right thing to do."

He hung up. I felt a little bit better. He sounded like he meant it.

"Lord," I prayed, "I feel helpless here, crippled and so far away from him. Give him wisdom"

Katy sat nearby, listening to this whole conversation. She was thirteen years old.

I found out later that he had sent the kids back to Zacatecas and gone with her to Las Vegas.

Before long, Rory left Marta in a hotel in Las Vegas and came up to Minnesota; the first one of several trips made over the next few months. He came to see me. I'll never forget that meeting. He came in and began to cry. I was still mostly bed-ridden. He sat there by my bed, tears running down his face, saying over and over how sorry he was. I told him it was all right, that I knew he had not driven off the road on purpose. I told him I knew it was an accident. He never came out and said it in words, but it didn't seem like it was my injuries he was sorry about. He left me in a state of confusion. I had felt no indication of love or care from him. It felt like what he had come for was to ease his own conscience by, at least, making the trip to see me in person. He did not have the courage to come out and tell me what he was planning to do. If he had, I'm not sure if that would have been better or not. Rory left again and I didn't hear anything from him for a while. I'm not sure where he went, but then he came back to Minnesota. I heard he was around, but thought he was by himself. It puzzled me that he didn't come to see me.

Then he left again. He phoned and told me he'd found a job in Las Vegas doing rigging again. Not true, of course, but I believed him.

I was hopeful, but clueless. I was happy and content, so sure that I would walk again and we'd all go back to Zacatecas together.

Chapter 23

August 1988

They did get me up and walking in a custom fitted fiberglass cast. I was in pain unless I was lying down flat but I could be up and around. That, to me, was the most important part. I had to achieve that ability and more in order to be discharged from the hospital.

By September, we were in a house just in time for the kids to start school. It seemed like things were going in a positive direction. Then, in October, something new.

I began to feel pain in my lower abdomen. There had been so much trauma and damage that there was a tendency to chalk it up as residual; more of the same. When the pain grew to where it was making me scream, the doctors realized it might be some new problem; something not associated with the accident. After making a thorough examination, it was determined that my fallopian tubes had become twisted and they had not found it early enough. Too much time had passed. They were already gangrenous. Emergency surgery was required. Once into surgery, it was clear that the condition had come close to being fatal. They estimated that I was only an hour from dying. I, of course, had no idea of how critical it was, but when they told me, it was like, "Really? My, my." This near-death stuff was getting to be monotonous.

With the body cast, I had achieved some modest mobility. After this latest surgery, the cast was too painful. My back was still too weak to carry me upright, so I was bedridden once again.

By Christmas, I was able to stand the body cast and so, could begin therapy. Muscles atrophy, of course, when not being used. Those muscles needed to be built back up. If you have never gone through that process, be glad. It was not a piece of cake. Rory was home for a brief period over the holidays, but did not have much to say. Over the next few months, he sent money for rent once or twice, usually late. That was a hard time, as we often had no money for groceries. It was also a growing time; praying in the money for our needs. Rory, during that time, still called nearly every night.

Within another year, I attempted life without the support of that body cast. It was another chapter of painful adaptation, but a necessary chapter if I was ever going to get to a place of near-normalcy.

Rory was back in Minnesota at this time working for my nephew, Eric. Rory had a way about him. People liked him and he gravitated to relatives for employment.

Somebody wrote a country song based on a spiritual maxim that sang my life.

"One day at a time, sweet Jesus…Give me the strength to do everything that I need to do.

Yesterday's gone, and tomorrow may never be mine.

Help me today, show me the way, one day at a time."

That's the way I lived. That's the way we should all live, all the time, of course. But my situation made that life-approach an absolute necessity. Each day came and went, but I could never get very far away from thoughts of where Rory was and what he was doing.

May 1989

As I have related, Rory had long had a problem with gambling, but had kept it out of his life while on the mission field. Now unconstrained, that problem took root and he began to gamble as a serious pastime. He honestly believed that he could solve his money problems by winning in the casinos. Before long, all our credit cards were maxed out and we were forced to file for bankruptcy. The medical bills were staggering. Amazingly, the hospitals saw fit to forgive what was owed. We still owned our house in Minnesota and had been renting it out. There was some equity there so we sold it and were able to repay personal loans we had gotten from friends and relatives.

It was one sad scenario after another. We were swept along in a downward spiral that seemed to be our lives. Days were endurable because there was so much to attend to. Activity helps push depression back. But nights were hard.

Despair and depression were fairly normal human responses to the onslaught of events and our enemy, the devil, knows how and when to get at us most successfully. I was never again tempted by thoughts of suicide, but went through my days feeling pretty lost and alone unless I kept my eyes on the Lord and worked on keeping things together for the kids. I watched them and looked for signs of damage.

My oldest girl, my sweet Anissa, seemed to be bearing up pretty well. It probably actually helped that she was the oldest and knew she was expected to oversee the other two. She kept up in school and looked for ways to help me without being asked. She was developing a kind of inner strength that would grow to make her a leader with influence. Anissa was becoming a tough little girl.

Rory John was just a kid during this time. Handsome and smart, Rory adapted quickly to any situation. Most of the time, he seemed to be dealing with things in a good way. Beneath the surface though, he was seething with anger and bitterness. Somehow, he knew far more than I did what was happening and knew it long before I had much of an inkling. He consistently kept the reality of what was going on clear in his own mind, but, on occasion, brought it to me. He loved his dad, but had a violent hatred for everything his dad was doing. He began to pull away from the things of God. He was hoping for things to turn around, but the longer this travesty continued, the harder his heart became. He was creating a kind of shell to keep from feeling the hurt in his heart. We talked often, but I could see how conflicted he was.

And Katy. This little creature of ours. Katy was our family barometer. She had and still has, a sensitivity that gives her insight into things that regular folks never see. Back in Mexico and all through this horror, Katy had seen and reported on every aberration in her dad's behavior. Katy had a solid sense of what was right and would not be rationalized out of taking a firm stand. When all of the rest of us were willing to look the other way and give things the benefit of a doubt, Katy stuck out her chin and said no. She was the boldest of all, this little thing, in confronting her dad with the truth. I had already been in the hospital in Minnesota when she finally convinced her brother that something had to be done. He agreed and told Katy to tell Anissa. Anissa immediately said they should go right to dad and get it straightened out. Anissa told me many years later that the three of them went to talk to him. Anissa explained that Katy had overheard him talking on the phone late at night and was worried.

"I was talking to your mother," he said. "I don't want to hear any more about it now. That subject is closed."

Katy in her little girl's voice said "You don't tell mom you love her in Spanish."

He got violently angry, then and called her terrible names. So angry he almost came to the point of physical assault – but she stood there unflinching. He never struck her. He knew she was right. What an amazing little girl.

January 1989

At that time, my brother John offered Rory a job working with him out in California. We owed such an enormous amount of money that the debt was frightening. In fact, I could only keep from being paralyzed at the thought of it by forcing my mind away. Rory told me he thought he could make more money out there than working construction during a Minnesota winter. I still couldn't sign my name due to the trauma but we got a checking account opened with which Anissa helped me all during her senior year. Rory was acting so strange, though, that I thought being with my brother Johnny might be a help to him. Johnny told me he thought that Rory was feeling very guilty. He felt that was why Rory's actions were so odd and inexplicable. He and Rory shared a motel room for a time and Johnny was puzzled by the long, middle-of-the-night walks Rory took. Rory explained that he slept better after.

Rory left for California in 1989 and stayed more than a year. He worked, gambled and, unbeknownst to my brother or anyone else, stayed with Marta. During that time, I put my efforts toward returning to a semblance of normalcy, practicing writing and processing events and ideas in sequence, something that my injuries had made difficult. I began to realize a little how insanity must feel. My brain would not follow things in a consecutive way, but would from time to time, "jump the tracks."

I had terrifying nightmares almost every night. My healing was intimidated by the sleep I lost. The Christian psychologist I had been mandated to see since I had suffered head injuries had told me that the nightmares I was having probably had a lot to do with the fact that in a practical sense I had lost my entire life in that accident. Those nightmares felt so real and were so terrifying. They were a result, the doctor said of having lost my home, my children because they were, by necessity, living with relatives, and my husband who seemed like a stranger because his behavior was so strange and indifferent. The doctor felt that being able to return to Zacatecas to say goodbye to the church and the people we loved would be a big help.

It turned out he was right about that.

Rory had been up to spend some time with us and was planning to go back to California the same day that the kids and I were going to make the trip to Mexico. My sweet little sister Kathy had agreed to drive us all back to Zacatecas in her van. Kathy's van was roomy and equipped with a mattress in the back so I could rest when needed. The trip went smoothly and being back to what felt like home was good medicine. We were able to stay in a house right across the street from the one we lived in before the accident. I was invited to visit the house in which we had lived to see how it looked with the new occupants. We were also able to attend a service at our church. The ministry was running well under our wonderful friend Chuy's capable leadership. The kids got to see their friends and say good-bye again. We also got to visit several friend's homes and I saw bits and pieces of my life every place we went. A piece of décor here or a cook pot there; it was strangely comforting. The nightmares stopped.

The trip was a blessing and I was so grateful to my dear sister. She also interrupted her life and moved back from New England that year to live with us. She had worked as a campaign director of New England for President George HW Bush. I'm sure it was a sacrifice because she was very involved in politics at that time.

We came back to an empty house but the kids all got right back into school and sports. I practiced writing – getting my skills back you know - and with a little help I could get propped up against the sink to wash dishes. Little things like that helped me feel a bit more normal. It was, usually Anissa who would take me to the school on basketball game days. They would park me on the side of the gym floor and I would sit through not one but four games. Both Katy and Rory John played both JV and Varsity. Kids love having parents there to watch them perform and parents love to be there. I sure did.

Those were very good days. I got to know other parents and my kid's friends and that was so very important to me.

I was offered the position of heading up a new Spanish program at Maranatha Christian Academy where my kids had been attending on scholarships. Because it was the first time it was offered, I would only have to work part time. I remember that I still had to move around in a wheel chair when the principal, Mr. Sullivan met with me. In spite of my severely handicapped condition, he still wanted me to do it. My kids were happy in school and although Anissa graduated that year, I saw this as the only way I could keep Rory John and Katy in that wonderful Christian school. I agreed and their tuition was my pay for that year.

I was a bit hesitant that first day. I'd been able to choose the books and system with which I felt comfortable, but being back in a class room was one thing. Being there in a full body brace was quite another. That was daunting.

I fell right into it, daunting or not. I love teaching and I loved the students and the staff! I always had Mexico at the back of my mind, though. This job was very much another "God thing." The trauma of the accident had caused some long-term memory loss and my Spanish had suffered as a result. Before the accident, I was able to converse and write pretty well. Now, a lot of it was just gone.

Teaching Spanish and going back to square one for the basics helped bring it all back. My fluency might have been better before than now, but I can chalk that up to ten years difference in age.

Rory was back in Minnesota again. He slept at our own house and was trying to find work. The kids and I were living at my brother, John's house in Orono, a nice western suburb of the Twin Cities, that first year out of the hospital. It had a first floor bed and bath so I only had to climb the steps to take showers.

That next year we moved into an apartment set up for the handicapped. Very nice and much closer to the school. Things felt pretty good. Time passed.

Chapter 24

February 1991

I had such a longing for Mexico. I asked the Lord over and over why I had to stay while others didn't even want to go. I really *wanted* to go. My kid's missed it, too. Their dad was around off and on but no longer a very big part of their lives.

I prayed and, bit by bit, God was answering. The missions club had a trip planned to Haiti and because of a coup the airport was closed. Brian Sullivan, our principal there at Maranatha, asked me if I thought I could work something out for a trip to Mexico instead.

I quickly called our good friends, Paul and Kathy Cagle who were living and working in and around Acapulco. They said they'd help in any way they could, so in just a couple of weeks we had a plan worked out and 13 young students were excited and planning to be on the team. The oldest was a junior. I worked with the kids and so did Cheryl Theisen, the gym and health teacher. I was surely blessed with her! She did the majority of the work, actual accounting, etc. We were scheduled to go over Easter vacation that year.

I was so thrilled to be able to do this and just get back into doing something, reaching the lost! The night before we left we had a packing party with all of the parents. All of the students brought things to give away for the ministry there.

At the end I shared with them the importance of prayer and must have gotten a little carried away; preaching. Well, sharing my heart anyway.

One of the dads, who was also the youth pastor came up to me and simply said "Lee Anne, what are you doing here? Sitting here listening to all you're saying and the way you're saying it, you are obviously called to Mexico.!" I stammered, hemmed and hawed a bit and said, "Well, I'm still healing, we still owe a lot of money, umm, umm, umm." I felt awful!

I went to bed that night crying out to the Lord, "What do you want from me? You know I want to go and I'm trapped. My husband doesn't even act like a Christian anymore! But You called me! Why!?" I was trying to pray. I was trying to "Count it all joy." I couldn't find it in me. I was still in the body cast. I was still in constant pain.

"It's too much, Lord. I am so badly hurt! I am losing everything!"

I realized I had begun to shout. There was anger and fear in my heart and it could be heard. I knew better, but I went ahead and vented my frustration and rage and aimed it at my creator – my

Lord and my Savior. Then something happened. Something that had never happened to me before. He spoke to me. Not in my mind or in my spirit, He spoke in an audible voice.

People are often a little glib about God telling them things. "I was asking God about what I should do and He told me to move to California," they might say. Or, to some unsuspecting young lady, " God told me that you were going to be my wife.." or, "God said I should quit my job, leave my family and become an itinerant evangelist." Or whatever. This kind of thing has a very spiritual sound to it, and also has the quality of being unquestionable. Where you might want to respond with; "He did not!" what are you going to use for an argument? And there's always the possibility of their experience being real. I admit to being somewhat skeptical at times, but I know we can always look to Him for direction and comfort and we can receive it. He loves us. He is sending a constant stream of communication, most of which we have no ears to hear. Most often though, I believe He speaks to us through His Word. We experience the supernatural direction and instruction of a loving God because His Holy Spirit breathes life into a passage of scripture that speaks straight to your heart. Certainly every Christian has had this wonderful kind of revelation. It ought to be a regular occurrence.

This was more. This was so amazing; so dramatic! And just one sentence; He said, out loud, **"I am going to set you free!"**

God's promise of freedom is there for every one of us. We can be made free by the knowledge of the truth, His word says. Not just free. Free with an emphasis; "Free, indeed!" God knows what we need and never presses us beyond what we can handle. This "out loud" proclamation gave me hope and filled me with faith. I was stunned into silence and immediately felt remorseful. I had just been angrily denouncing the God of Abraham, Isaac and Jacob; the creator of the universe and He responded in this incredible, miraculous, loving way. Who was I to be given this amazing gift? I finally collected myself and began to praise and worship Him. This word was set firmly in my spirit. It would be put to the test in the days and weeks to come, but that was why He did it for me. The tests would be hard.

Being the type of person I am, I immediately called Anissa and said, "Everything is going to be okay. Dad is going to be fine and we're all going back to Mexico soon! God told me." Notice…that is not what God said at all. He had simply said "I'm going to set you free". I made up my own hopeful interpretation.

Chapter 25

April 1991

I left on that trip to Mexico, feeling like I was on eagle's wings. I was so excited. During the time we had there in what was, to them a foreign land, the kids threw themselves into enthusiastic ministry. What they accomplished was awe-inspiring. They got to pray with hundreds of people in Spanish and in English too, as there were so many Americans on the beaches where we did our skits and puppet shows. I came home still on the wing emotionally. I couldn't wait to tell Rory all about it. I just knew he was going to be as excited as I was when he heard about everything that had happened.

But my husband didn't show at the airport. My son was there instead. He was standing, waiting, with his teeth clenched. I could tell he was furious. I asked him where his dad was. He started to answer but with such an angry tone I told him to wait till we could talk in the car.

Once settled, he blew up. "Mother, you're an idiot! Dad is having an affair and you walk around like everything is peachy."

"Oh no, darling, Dad might be gambling but I am pretty sure that he would never have an affair," I said in a pleading voice.

He was so angry that he started to cry. "He has not been home this entire week! He called me and told me to pick you up tonight. He is with someone. He has not been home," he repeated. "You are living in a dream world. You're so dumb!" This from my darling son, who had never sassed me or said a disrespectful word to me in his life. He was furious and frustrated because I didn't believe him.

I went to bed without my husband again that night. I still had my "promise" and my heart was expectant. He showed up at 5:00 am. He made no excuse. He had nothing to say.

May 1991

We had a good friend, actually a brother of Rory's step-mother, so more like family to us. His name was Gordon Peterson. In their teens, Rory and Gordy had been best friends. We had been married in his dad's church. Rory asked me if I'd be willing to go see Gordon the next day. Of course, I said yes! This must be the first step, I thought. Rory told me he'd pick me up after school to take me there.

Gordy pastored a church that had been a steady supporter of our ministry in Mexico. Rory told me he had spent some time with Gordy and there were some things we needed to discuss. I was confused, but a little encouraged. The fact that Rory was seeing someone that could offer spiritual counsel and insight to what we were going through gave me a bit of hope. We showed up at the appointed time.

"Come on in, Lee Anne," Gordy said. He was trying to smile, but I could see it was a try and not really how he felt. "Let's go into my study."

Gordy's study was a good-sized room with a desk by the window, a sofa and a few chairs. Family photographs filled one wall and a large oil painting hung across from them. When we came in, Rory went and sat down in a chair at one side. Gordy asked me to take a seat on the sofa on the other side. Rory was sitting forward, his elbows on his knees. His hands were clasped and he looked stressed and unhappy.

Gordy stayed standing and began to pace.

"Lee Anne, I'll just get right to it. Rory has confessed to having an affair with this Mexican woman. She is here in town. He has been keeping her at a motel just a mile from your apartment." I was shocked. What in the world? I started to feel sick.

"He married her in Las Vegas, but of course, that marriage was not legal. He was married to you." He had "married" her early on in this parody of a relationship in order to add to ways to keep her in the states, Gordy said tersely. When I heard that, I was crushed and dismayed. He had not divorced me, so he was breaking even more laws. I guess I could have contacted the authorities. But what good would it have done for me to try to make an issue of it?

An affair…and an illegal marriage. One stunning blow after another. I was reeling with the impact of every new revelation.

Rory sat quietly, looking at the floor. He wouldn't lift his eyes and look at me.

Gordy went on. "Rory says it's over and done with. He and I will go and put her on a bus back to Mexico right away."

Still not a word from Rory. I was speechless. I know my mouth must have been hanging open. What I was hearing was so mind-numbing I couldn't put thoughts together. *No, God*, I was thinking. *You said it would be fine*. I tried to tell Gordy what God had said to me, but couldn't get the words out. The only thing that sounded remotely good was the promise that it was over. How I wish that had been true.

Gordy went on to tell me that Rory thought he might have given me a venereal disease. Gordy wanted me to go straight to a doctor. This awful scene just kept getting worse. I couldn't process it. I was literally overwhelmed. Nausea surged in me. I started to vomit and went quickly to the bathroom.

When I came back into the room Gordon had one more thing to say. "Rory took that woman and her children illegally into the US. He is now wanted for kidnapping in Mexico. He'll never be able to go back into that country."

The one hope I had held onto during this seemingly unending nightmare was that we would all be back on the mission field in Mexico again – that our work would not be lost – that I would have my husband back and we would go on serving the Lord together. And now he was a wanted criminal?

That felt like the final straw. I knew that God could heal and restore; I knew He could do anything… but this?

While Gordon kept talking, I saw Rory slip to his knees from the chair and begin to weep. He kept saying he was sorry, repeating it over and over. I know he was sorry. Now it appears to have been the kind of sorry that a person feels emotionally, but just not a Godly kind of sorry that leads to repentance. My world had just crumbled…again. I felt empty and numb. What possible future was there for me…for us?

Gordy then went on to tell me the reason Rory had gone to him. Rory had an addiction to gambling. The wide-spread emergence of Indian casinos had legitimized that kind of thing in many people's minds. For Rory, that quasi-legitimacy made it almost irresistible. He would win from time to time and get the idea that he was good at it, but most of the time, he'd keep playing till whatever winnings he had would be gone. Now, he'd been gambling again and had lost his whole check. My paycheck had come in the mail while I was in Mexico and he had cashed and lost that as well. Our rent was due in 5 days. Gordon told me not to worry about that. He said that he would cover it for us and continued talking about how Rory would stay in their basement until he, Gordy, was satisfied Rory was free. His words were coming at me and everything sounded so bizarre and horrible, but, I knew! I knew I had heard from God. My heart told me that the only way for me to be free like He told me I would be was if Rory was released from this woman's spell. This was not a conscious thought-out process. It felt like a heart knowing. It was a heart's desire. But it was just a hope, and it was wrong.

I interrupted Gordy. I told him that God had already spoken to me about this and that Rory could come home with me. I was prepared, I told him. I wasn't, though. I wasn't prepared at all.

We got in the car and left for our house. As we drove away, I let go of my thoughts for a bit and felt some level of peace. Then, Gordy's words pushed back into my mind and I began to cry again. Rory drove silently, but reached over from time to time to put a hand on my knee.

For the next two days Rory was late coming home from work because he was out with Gordon looking for Marta so they could put her on a bus. Rory told me they couldn't find her. She had left the motel. The desk lady said some people had picked her up. Rory thought she didn't know anyone in Minneapolis. Later we found out she had contacted a women's shelter. She was pretty good at telling stories and they evidently took her at her word.

The third day Rory was different. The minute he walked in the door I knew something had gone wrong. "She called me at work," he said abruptly, without looking me in the face. "She needs to see me. I have to go help her get back to Mexico."

"Take Gordy", I pleaded. He ignored me.

"He's a busy man, Lee Anne. I can take care of this. I'm going."

I am confident that if he had involved Gordy at this point, she would, indeed have been put on the bus and been on her way back. It probably made little difference. I am pretty sure that if Marta had been able to contact Rory in any way, even from Mexico, he would have made it his business to "rescue" her again. A definite pattern was firmly in place.

He was gone for a short time and then came back again. "She is pregnant, Lee Anne. I am the father. I have to help her." He started to pack a few things. My mind was reeling. I knew she said she had been bleeding heavily before the accident. She had been in and out of the hospital several times with self-inflicted injuries. We had prayed for her. I was wondered if that bleeding might have been the result of a botched abortion. She had been trying to get my husband to take her away back then and she must have known it would be hard to get him to take her if she was pregnant. Now, she evidently believed he would stay because she was.

He left. I didn't even cry.

He came back the next day. "Marta had a miscarriage," he told me. He went back to work the next day as if things were normal. When he got home from work he informed me that she was having twins and that she only lost one. She was still pregnant, she had told him. I began to wonder if he was that gullible or just being willfully stupid. I argued with him about it but he said he had to go to her. I took him back six times in all during this crazy ordeal. Finally even Gordy said that I had to let him go. But, he was so worth saving! I know during those years that I prayed for him so much; almost to the exclusion of anything or anyone else. To my everlasting dismay, I know I must have prayed more for him than for our children. I regret that so very much.

Chapter 26

What makes a man do it? What amazing contortions does his mind have to make in order to take that road?

The strange thing is how often this kind of craziness appears to happen. Maybe it's just the jarring incongruity that makes these excursions into the dark become so interesting and fascinating. The renowned and revered spiritual leader suddenly (but maybe not that suddenly) caught in an affair with a secretary or deacon's wife and departing in disgrace from a life and ministry that had touched thousands, and if not interrupted in this insane way, would surely have touched thousands more.

Thinking more about that, I imagine a marriage gone cold must have something to do with it. That, and maybe an abandonment of sound practice, the circumspect behavior of a wise man when it comes to contact with the opposite sex. In some men, there may be an arrogance that gives them the warped idea that the rules don't apply to them. If there is a weakness in that area, foolish behavior opens doors. Certainly, in the married ones, a pulling apart and cessation of the kind of communication that helps keep couples on the "straight and narrow" but becomes conversation kept to the impersonal and mundane. A relationship, where thoughts and motives become guarded. Where secrets are kept from each other. Lives lived in emotional separation. With us, though, that did not seem to be the case. We were close and had a healthy sex life. We talked about everything; even the most intimate. There was a secret he was keeping, but there was never even a hint of that dark side he kept hidden. Embarrassment or shame and the counsel of our enemy, Satan, will keep a person silent about sexual sin. Sin, kept in the dark, has far more power and strength to bind us than if we bring it out into the light. The Word directs us to confess our faults and failings to each other and when we do that, that open confession brings healing. This is an amazingly powerful principle. The only way it will ever happen, though, is if you really want to be free.

Early in our preparation for the ministry we took some classes on counseling. I remember hearing that men should never counsel a woman alone or behind a closed door. The same thing applied to women. They should not counsel a man alone. It made sense. We never even discussed the wisdom of that practice. It was self-evident.

From the time we started working with our cell group in our home in Minnesota, Rory never, ever counseled a woman alone. Then we followed the same policy on the farm in Minnesota, and subsequently when we got to Mexico. Whenever a woman wanted counseling, young or old, Rory always had me with him in his office or else brought the person into the kitchen. He would sit in the kitchen nook, in between the working kitchen and the dining room where the kids were studying and within our hearing. Things of a confidential nature were discussed in hushed voices. If the counselee felt uncomfortable, we both would go back to his office where the door could be closed. Wherever it was, I could join him and I always did just that. He felt a women's perspective was often critical. Often, he would involve me by just asking me to pray.

I am often asked how it happened. That safeguard…how did it break down? I believe that the first time he convinced himself it was alright to meet Marta alone was the beginning of the end for him. He told me later it was because she told him she couldn't trust me after I fired her and, to him, she seemed to need help so badly. In his mind, he was the only one who could help her. Listening to the lies of the enemy has to be that first slip down the slippery slope.

Lust, I suppose, might typically be part of it. Many women; silly women the Bible calls them, are attracted to men in positions of power and authority; like female animals, seeking mates that show strength.

In the Christian realm, we need to always be on the alert. It must be recognized that our enemy, Satan is always doing his best to bring marriages and ministries to ruin.

But, as the Word of God is careful to warn, we are tempted when we are led away by our own lusts and enticed. Our closest and most relentless enemy is our flesh – our human selves. Paul said he needed to put his flesh to death every single day. Left alive, our human carnal side will do the opposite of what is right.

I can't find it in myself to be harshly judgmental with Rory. I've been hurt – hurt badly – but, as Jesus said; "If you are without sin of your own, go ahead and throw that stone" I forgave Rory long ago and told him so. There is plenty of sin in my history – but, it's so wonderful to be forgiven and His word says God can't forgive me if I hold unforgiveness in my own heart.

Where was the chink in Rory's armor? Was his departure from the Lord sudden or gradual? He had so many reasons for "staying the course."

A faithful, loving wife.

Three terrific kids.

A ministry – maybe not thriving, Billy Graham style – but fruitful and effective.

Marta's conversion. Her husband and children as well.

A strong support system – prayer and finances.

And Jesus, comforter and friend who, with the Holy Spirit provided every single thing needed to persevere and succeed – there are no excuses.

What did Marta bring that I couldn't offer?

I loved him – She adored him.

I looked to him for headship and strength – She needed him desperately and was able to talk and act in a way that made him believe it. Was her need augmented by a desire to get to America and have the storied better life for her kids? If so, it must have seemed to her that Rory was the likeliest avenue to that end.

Was she beautiful? Everyone who knew her would say not. She was quite plain – not ugly, but not beautiful either.

What she brought to the relationship with Rory were problems.

She was married.

She had children.

She had no money.

If she left her husband and took her children along, Rory could be charged with kidnapping. That actually became the case and for many years, Rory could not enter Mexico without risking arrest.

If she did enter the U.S. she would be doing so illegally.

All in all, there was very little in this line of reasoning that helps explain Rory's apostasy. He almost made the break from disaster. His tearful repentance on the road to the border just before the accident was sincere, I believe.

I keep coming back to the spiritual battle that was being waged. That must have been a real barn-burner. We know it's always going on, but don't always see it so clearly. As far as Rory's out-of-character behavior, I have to take the spell and the curse into account. For our experience, it seems to be a definite factor. There are some things to ponder, though if I want to follow that trail.

One: We believe that, as God's children, we are safe from that kind of attack. After all, how can a smelly old witch-doctor conjure up something stronger than God? Answer? He can't! That nasty devil-filled rascal is probably comfortable in the belief that his "magic" is his – a gift from pagan gods. He is, no doubt, blissfully unaware that whatever his incantations and potions bring about, he, like all creation, is able to do only what Almighty God permits. Job's boils – my broken self and my entire physical condition.

Knowing that makes even the curse more bearable. Job just kept on trusting. Lee Anne, with occasional lapses, did the same. Job got recompensed and got a chapter in the Bible. My story is not over yet, but so far, so good. Too late for a chapter in the Bible, but I do have a mansion waiting for me.

Now, the spell.

From Marta's point of view, she probably chose to see it as a blessing. She needed him to love her and to leave me. She didn't just ask and trust. She paid good money; missions money… money God's people had sent to help further the work of the Kingdom. In the world's way of dealing with things – (and the Bible seems to agree; See Ecclesiastes "money answers all things") her "faith", the faith she placed in money and magic, had to help things along.

So, is there such a spell? A spell that could bind a believer? A believer inhabited by God's Holy Spirit?

To every observer close to us, that's how it appeared. Rory was, apparently, spell-bound. Every move – every decision he made went counter to even basic common sense, and certainly counter to the direction of the Lord. In the midst of his bewitching, I prayed harder and sought God more than at any other time in my life. I know I was praying in the right direction. That focus brought a closeness to Jesus I hadn't had before.

I can't say for sure, but at some point, probably after the accident, Rory must have said a final "okay" to the outlandish ideas spinning around in his brain. Can a spell cast on a Christian work? Is it that much different than some more mundane temptation? That born-again child of God looks away from God's promised escape hatch and focuses instead on that sparkly, twinkly, fascinating sin. But without that inclination, the temptation, or in this case, the spell, is powerless.

There's an old horror story that is an excellent allegory for the way God's laws and principles work. It's called; "The Monkeys Paw." In the story, the paw grants wishes when held in the wisher's hand. Every wish is granted, but in a way that has ghastly aspects. God will step back and let you have whatever you stubbornly demand. You'll have it and wish you had never asked. The Israelites grew bored with a steady diet of manna. God gave them what they craved and it made them sick. How wise and safe it is to make it your business to find out what God wants for you and then go after that with all your heart. How stupid and prideful it is to believe that your personal, selfish desires will satisfy and fulfill you.

Under that spell, Rory became an outlaw. He lied to his friends and his family and he lived a lie. He lost his life; first to shame and mediocrity, then to sickness and helpless dependence. He has so much time these days to think and so much to regret. His only solace; that his children still love him. They love him, but have lost respect for him. Their father is pitiful in their eyes. I talk to him from time to time. He just cries and says he's sorry.

And Marta? Older and plumper, but still here living in America. She has a menial job and comes home to a bed-ridden old man that requires help with every part of his life. I have forgiven her as well and wish and pray good things for her.

One thing I really believe. Given another chance, my sweet Rory would, this time opt for God's best. But then…wouldn't we all?

Bill and Gloria Gaither wrote a musical back in the eighties that had such a great message. The idea was that God, himself, is the source of music. "God gave the song. His name is Jesus" I know every believer is helped and inspired by God's music. For me, His music has comforted, sustained and motivated me through every aspect of my life. I love to have it around me. It's wonderful in my private prayer time.

Some songwriters become truly anointed to bring spiritual nourishment to weary souls. One; Laura Story – wrote these words and put them to a beautiful melody.

We pray for wisdom, Your voice to hear
We cry in anger when we cannot feel You near
We doubt your goodness, we doubt your love
As if every promise from Your word is not enough
And all the while, You hear each desperate plea
And long that we'd have faith to believe
Then that

chorus:

'Cause what if your blessings come through rain drops
What if Your healing comes through tears
What if a thousand sleepless nights are what it takes to know You're near
What if trials of this life are Your mercies in disguise

What if, indeed?

According to the word of God, marriage is "till death do you part." Almost anyone that has gone through divorce is forced to admit that although they no longer live with their ex and have even gone on to marry someone else, the connection that keeps them from parting still remains. Only after one of them physically dies, can the other feel the release of that connection.

In my case, I have a connection with Rory. It shows itself in sudden flashbacks of memory. I'll be watching television or sitting in a church service when I'll get a mental picture of a time past. Us on a vacation. The family around the table at dinner. Rory preaching. Him holding me close. Then I'll feel fresh again the sense of loss. I'll ask again; why? And then I'll turn away and look ahead. "No one, having put their hand to the plow and looks back is worthy of the kingdom," Jesus said.

Chapter 27

July 1991

Rory left for good that summer. He had come and gone so many times that the whole situation had become nothing more than a cheap charade. Our friend, Gordy, had told me before this that it was time to recognize the reality of the decision Rory had made. Our last trip as a family was to go to Dallas for Anissa's graduation from Christ for the Nations, a Christian college in Texas. We would have been better off not pushing for him to go. Rory was cold and mean. It was a pretty horrible time for all of us.

When we got back to Minnesota, Rory got packed up and ready to leave. I had left my rings on his alarm clock. He put them off to one side and took the clock. I think he knew the double life was about to end and appeared to be feeling bad about it. He was leaving so all of the lying and sneaking would no longer be necessary. That being the case, he could spare a little niceness, acting sorrowful and telling me he loved me and wished our marriage wasn't over. He kissed me goodbye. I don't remember crying.

Time passed and life went on.

September; 1991

Healthwise, everything seemed to be progressing nicely when one of my legs started failing. It would get weak and buckle under me. I nearly had what would surely have been disastrous falls several times before I got to the doctor. They were not sure of what was causing this, but began a series of tests to try to find out.

I was so tired of doctors and hospitals by this time. It seemed like my life consisted of one appointment after another – test after test. Please don't misunderstand, I was grateful to be cared for and some of those people were honestly kind and had a sincere interest in me and my recovery. Many times, health care professionals become inured to the pain and trauma that makes up their daily life. That is usually a sort of natural process that allows them to go home at the end of their day and leave it all behind. I love the fact that I have a number of true friends today that were my doctors and care-givers back then. Friends that never left me behind.

As the fall continued, other events began to transpire. I waited for the outcome of the tests.

While they were still trying to sort out the problem with my leg, I went in for an eye exam. Eye problems, even blindness can result from Juvenile diabetes. As time passes, it is prudent to check things out.

I first met with the head of that clinic. He worked with a lot of diabetics and was considered an expert in the field. The exam was pretty arduous as I had that cumbersome back brace and couldn't get good readings without the equipment or my chair being adjusted just so. I had to be taken to one room after another to get it all done. By the time all the tests had been administered, I was weary, to say the least. I had been there for more than four hours. When it was over, the doctor called me in, picked up a chart and began to tear another part of my life into little pieces.

"Lee Anne, I have something to tell you…" From his tone, it was clear that whatever he was seeing in that chart was not good news. He began, in a very soft voice, to tell me that my eyes had begun to deteriorate at the back; at the optic nerve. He said he had been so pleased that he had always found my eyes to be healthy, especially in light of the fact that I had had Juvenile Diabetes for so long. I sat and waited, chewing on my bottom lip as he continued by explaining that there was no way to deal with it medically; no surgery or medicine. His face told me as much as his words just how bad he felt. I didn't try to argue or cry out for a second opinion. I just sat there as he finished by telling me he expected my sight would be gone – I'd be blind – by Christmas. He was so gentle and caring. He told me he would be praying for me. I was worn out already. This information just put me in a daze.

Blind? Already crippled up pretty badly, but blind? Excuse me, Lord, but what's up with this? Do I start learning Braille?

In that same time frame, actually just two days later, I had a mammogram; a routine part of my very regular checkups. They look at those on the spot, so I went right in to the office to see the doctor. Once again, a grave tone of voice.

"The films we took are back," he said. "They don't look as good as we had hoped. They show tumors are developing. I'm not saying the tests are conclusive, Lee Anne, but we see this kind of thing a lot and you should prepare yourself for the strong possibility that you will have to undergo a complete mastectomy. We have already made an appointment for you with the best surgeon I know." He was wringing his hands in obvious distress as he spoke.

"My goodness," I exclaimed. "Cancer?"

"That's what the scan shows," the doctor replied. "It does look as if we have detected it soon enough to keep it from metastasizing…" He went on but I was having trouble hearing what he was saying. My heart was pounding and there was a roaring in my ears. I felt light-headed and thought I might faint.

"We'll be in touch in the next day or so," he was saying, "but it only makes sense to arrange surgery as soon as possible."

The thought of breast removal is a nightmare for most women. I knew other women who had gone through it. The ones I had heard talk about it made it sound not too terrible. Preferable to death, was the assumption. I tried to put it into perspective. Not such a big deal, I kept saying to myself.

Later that same day, I was back to my spine specialist for more X-rays of the damage to my spine. As I came in and sat down, that old story about the camel that was being loaded for a journey came to my mind. Not just the punchline, I thought about the story leading up to it. It was easy to picture. This poor camel being loaded with more than anyone had ever seen a camel carry. They added even more and the animal seemed capable. When the load got so heavy, they could hardly believe it, they stood back, scrutinized the situation and said, "That camel can carry still more," but added only a little at a time. Finally, the load was so high they needed a ladder to add to it. "One little thing more," they said and began to add one additional piece of straw at a time. All seemed well, but the last straw they put on the top of the load broke the camel's back.

The load on my own back was nearly unendurable already, both physically and emotionally. I was carrying it, but was the point of breaking near at hand? In my own strength, I was well past that point already. But, *"Come to me, all you who are weary and heavy laden, and I will give you rest."* Mother Theresa has been quoted as saying, and I paraphrase; "I know God only gives us as much as we can handle, but sometimes I wish he didn't think so much of me."

The doctors had been somewhat amazed at the extent of my recovery because of the extent of the damage. On this occasion, what seemed like the most recent of dozens of X-rays, MRI's and CAT scans brought the doctors to a grim conclusion.

Doctor K ushered me into his office and sat me down. He showed me where the part of my spine that had burst in the accident and had begun to ossify, harden and become brittle, had now broken into several pieces. One of those pieces was sliding in and out of my spinal column with every movement I made. He went on to tell me that the shard was causing my leg to randomly buckle.

"So, what are we going to do about it?" I asked. Surely there must be a way to deal with this, I felt.

"Lee Anne," he said, "We feel there's nothing we can do. No one is willing to do that kind of surgery. There is too strong a likelihood that it would cause complete paralysis. Please understand?"

"What will happen? Will it heal?"

"It has already progressed and we feel it will probably continue to do so. In order to prevent the damage that could be fatal or if not fatal, almost certainly leave you a paraplegic, you will need to get off your feet pretty soon."

"A wheelchair?" I said. "I'm going to be in a wheelchair? When? For how long?"

"I'm not saying you'll need to do that exactly. What I want you to understand is that your back is in precarious shape. This is a dangerous situation. We'll have to talk about how you should take care regarding the wrong kind of movement. Let's just plan to find ways to keep you off your feet. But, let's do that soon; before the end of the year, to be safe. It wouldn't be prudent to wait too long," he said gently. "I can't say for how long you would have to be that careful, but it could be for a long time. I'm sorry to say this, but even a wheelchair is not going to be a safe place. The only sure way to keep damage from progressing would be complete immobility." He was sitting on the edge of his desk, his legs crossed at the ankles. His assistant sat still, her face averted. No happy faces here.

"I'm telling you this because I don't want you to have false hopes. I'm trying to be fair to you. I'm sure you know this is not what anyone wants."

All I could think was how much "complete immobility" sounded like paralysis. Why not take the risk?

Doctor K was the one with whom I had spent hours talking about the Lord and my faith. I know I responded to him in some positive way. I really cared for him and wanted him to be saved so I know I "acted" like I had faith that day. I'm pretty sure it was just that; an act. His news was like a sledge hammer.

Was this the last straw?

I have no recollection of leaving the office or how I got home. I kept thinking of things; ordinary things I had to do. Stuff the kids needed. Groceries. Were we out of milk? It seemed like we were always out of milk. My brain went away from the bleak future that seemed so surely to lie before me and turned to mundane tasks; things to which I could actually attend. I was trying to feel less helpless.

I felt like I was supposed to keep serving God in Mexico. But how could I do that in the face of all these ridiculously horrible conditions? Serve God? Productive? Blind, breastless and in a wheelchair? And no husband? God, Help me!

I went home like an old horse goes to the barn; no thought of where home was, just automatically headed that way. I wandered in to the apartment and dropped my coat and purse.

I collapsed into a kitchen chair and looked numbly around the room. The sun shone in through a window over the sink. Its' rays caught dust motes that floated and danced in its' light. The world outside hadn't changed. My world, on the other hand, was undergoing huge alterations. That audible promise God gave me; maybe the translation was God telling me that heaven was the ultimate freedom. That didn't feel right, but maybe… All I could pray was; "Lord Jesus, I trust you." That verse we often default to in rough times came to mind. *"All things work together for good…"* Okay, God, I prayed. I love you and I'm pretty sure I'm one of those called according to your purpose. Bring it to pass. Whatever happens, Lord, You be glorified in it.

I remember getting a pretty good night's sleep – either because I was peaceful or because I was using sleep to escape; I'm not sure which.

Lee Anne Worre Risk

Chapter 28

A week or two went by and as the situation
deteriorated and hope diminished, I began to indulge in a little self-
pity. Why me?

I went to my room and began to work up an attitude. I spent
time going over my list of grievances and I loudly complained to
God about how badly I was being treated. I avoided thinking about
what my Savior had endured in my behalf, and just enjoyed a time
of feeling sad and hurt and betrayed. God must have been shaking
his head. The kids came home so I had to stifle my complaints.
Katy brought in the mail.

I lay on my bed and began going through the assorted bills and
advertisements. I wasn't feeling very optimistic, but somehow, in
the back of my mind, God's promise to set me free asserted itself.
Katy had mentioned there was a letter from Chuy. I left it
unopened.

Our good friend, Chuy, (pronounced chewy) wrote to me
regularly. Chuy was our Mexican brother and co-worker for the
kingdom. He loved us both and God had often used us to speak into
his life. Chuy was broken up over Rory's actions. There were some

that had become discouraged over Rory's failings, but Chuy refused to let his own ship flounder. He was such a faithful friend. He had a full life – plenty of things of which he had to take care of, but he took the time to try to encourage and comfort me. I liked his letters because they always included news and updates on the ministry. His letter arrived that day. The exact day this triple-whammy hit me. The same day I had been yelling at God. I opened it and began, somewhat listlessly, to read it. I found it to be typical of his usual letters. It was always short and on that flimsy, all-one-page airmail type paper. You wrote in it and then folded it up and mailed it. If it got wet, it disintegrated. It carried news and prayers and blessings. And a Bible verse. He always added a Bible verse when he closed. Just the reference, the book, chapter and verse; he never wrote out the words in the passage. The words were there in every Bible. Writing them out took space on the little paper on which he was writing. His favorites were passages from obscure parts of the Old Testament. Today was no different. Habbakuk; *obscure as ever*, I thought absently. As usual, I had no idea what the verse would be. I went back to complaining but, after reading all the newsy stuff, once again, decided to look it up. I had always looked them up before and they never made any sense to me. Just weird verses. Sometimes I looked them up in my Spanish Bible with the idea that it would be more understandable. That didn't usually help. I looked around and found my copy of the Amplified

Bible. It was always right there next to my bed. I loved that translation then and I love it still. I love the way how, in that version, every word is brought out and made clear; how the full meaning of the original Greek is exposed. I opened it and thumbed through to the passage. Habbakuk 3:17-19. I began to read.

"Though the fig tree does not blossom and there is no fruit on the vines, though the product of the olive fails and the fields yield no food, though the flock is cut off from the fold and there are no cattle in the stalls,"

You got that right, Habbakuk old boy. That's exactly where I'm at, I thought. *I have nothing going for me.*

"Yet will I rejoice in the Lord; I will exult in the victorious God of my salvation!"

That made me madder.

I stiffened. *I will not; No way, Jose, to put it in Mexican terms. I can't. At least not right now. Maybe later, Lord.*

Then that last verse:

"The Lord is my Strength, my personal bravery, and my invincible army; He makes my feet like hinds feet" – Here the words almost leapt from the page and a thrill ran up my spine – *"and will make me to walk (not to stand still in terror, but to walk) and make spiritual progress upon my high places (of trouble, suffering or responsibility)"*

Make me to Walk!! It was repeated! I read it over and over again.

Oh, the power of the Living Word of God. I was instantly transformed from a sniveling coward to a child of the Most High God. I knew then, in a fresh and fantastic way that HE was my strength; HE was my personal bravery; HE was my invincible army, and HE was going to MAKE me walk!

My friend had written this letter many days prior with no knowledge of the crisis by which my faith was being challenged. His choice of this particular passage at this particular time was clear evidence that he had been led by the Holy Spirit and that God was not yet through with me. So amazing!

I cried out to God for forgiveness. I had trusted Him for all these years and then lost confidence in the face of what seemed to be real. I had known before and now knew in a deeper way that what God says is real. Everything else is just mist and fog.

I would walk! I would not be pushed around in a wheelchair. Now, I knew it! That's what faith is; "the substance of things hoped for." And that's where it comes from. "By hearing" the Word says. When you hear God say He is going to do something, you know it is as good as done. When He says it, you can say it too. In fact, when we speak what God says, our words bring His will to life!

This time, He not only spoke with the words of an ancient prophet, He spoke through a humble servant at exactly the right time. What an amazing God!

For the first time in a long time, I began to experience the kind of peace that truly does pass understanding.

Lee Anne Worre Risk

Chapter 29

Back on the path

For believers, it's important to keep your spiritual eyes on the unseen. The visible stuff has no lasting reality. Only what happens in the Kingdom realm will last. We use doctors; so does God. But we need to always leave room for the supernatural. The God who made us is the God who can heal and restore. He is a promise-keeping God; a God of might and miracles.

Over the next few days, that God; my God; the God of the universe began to turn things around.

First, a call from the eye doctor.

After greeting him, he told me he had good news. I was in the mood for good news. He sounded cheerful and told me that when I had been there with him, he had picked up the wrong chart. He had another patient whose first name was very similar to mine. It was that poor lady who would soon be sightless. I know that was probably embarrassing for him, but I was jubilant. He sounded really happy, and went on and on about how great my eyes were and that I didn't even need a new prescription until I wanted to get new glasses.

"God bless you, doctor," I said. As he hung up the phone, I heard him clear his throat. He is a good man.

I hung up and sat for a while, trying to feel bad for the other patient. That poor other Leeann. It was almost like I had done it to her. I said a quick prayer for her and went to my thoughts on the life I had begun to build in my imagination. Thoughts I could now discard for good.

My mom had dealt with steady deterioration of her eyesight for years before she died. She had had an aneurism that nearly killed her and it had pressed on an optic nerve. The result for her was a kind of tunnel vision and it also made things blurry and indistinct. She loved Christian television, but had to sit very close. Near the end of her earthly life, she most often sat and listened to music and sermon tapes. Those sermons preached by her son, Dennis were her favorites. She never complained. She seemed impervious to frustration. I thought of her. So steady. So faithful. I thanked God again for the gift and example she was.

I had been trying to visualize how I would live without sight. I had accepted it – given it to the Lord. Now, He had given it back. Hallelujah! I have never again taken my eyesight for granted. What a precious gift, the ability to see.

My appointment with the Cancer surgeon was the next afternoon. They did some tests first and then another exam. This doc, a typical surgeon with not much in the "bed side manner" department, said, "This isn't cancer! What looked like malignancy to them are simply fibroid tumors…benign." "Really," I said. I was almost ready to take this crew to task. That first doctor had sat there in front of me and told me I would need to undergo a double mastectomy or else, die. No rational medical professional is ever totally sure about any diagnosis except, possibly a pronouncement of death, but there had been a note of professional certainty in his prognosis.

We mere mortals are all too prone to bestow full Godship on the medical community. We sit forward on our chairs, listen with credulous ears and take their prognosis, however dire straight to heart. I hope you realize that I am not suggesting that we never go to doctors. Not at all. As I said a bit ago, I'm simply stating that only God has the final word and we would be wise to always bear that in mind. He, God, is the best place to go to get that storied "second opinion." I say this now with the wisdom born of experience. I had accepted my fate and had been dreading the day when the surgery was to be performed. I just can't speak from any lofty, holier-than-thou position, is what I mean to say.

"Really?" I said again. "So, what about the surgery? Do these growths have to be removed?"

"In my experience, Lee Anne," he said, "none should be necessary. We'll check on things from time to time, but we are happy to have been wrong. Lay off the caffeine," he added, "that stimulates the growths." and walked out.

As I left his office I felt like doing a little pirouette. I was not quite yet at the point of doing something that strenuous, but I felt light. Look at this! I kept thinking. No mastectomy, no loss of sight and His promise; "I will make you to walk!" Wow, God!

The Lord was on the move. I was out of the pits and back in the race!

Chapter 30

I continued to have visits with Doctor K, a great doctor, my original orthopedist. He was a professed atheist and I humored him a little by not putting up too antagonistic of an argument, not reminding him of the fact that if there was no God, there would be no atheists. (Nobody to not believe in. Get it?) We had many long conversations and I believe that time we spent in conversation was never billed. In fact, I believe I never got a bill of any kind from this kind man. Doctor K always wanted to talk about the God he didn't believe in, creation versus evolution and other things of a spiritual nature. He was never abrasive or argumentative. He was honestly interested in me and in my relationship with Jesus.

When he heard the conversation we had with the accident investigator, he, with the investigator, was convinced that no one was strong enough to have held me back from going through the windshield. "Even if your husband was Atlas himself, he couldn't have done it!" I'm sure the thought was not in his mind, but he was making the case for a miracle. I jumped on it.

"Well," I said, "angels, then."

He stomped out of the room and we heard him say to the nurse; "Okay. Lee Anne just converted me. I was an atheist. Now, I guess I'm an agnostic. Maybe there is a God!" The nurses loved that.

The nay-sayers can never find a convincing argument against experience and relationship. There is none. "They overcame by the Blood of the Lamb and the word of their testimony." If we keep our relationship fresh, our testimony will always have the power to overcome. That's a great truth.

The day after my appointment and the devastating news that I was headed for a wheel chair, he called me. He set up the appointment with a plan to introduce an element of hope - which was interesting, since there had been nothing but gentle pessimism from him and his camp up to this point. Dr. K was worried about me. He wanted to find hope.

We met in his office; a small space with barely enough room for the chair I occupied. After very brief pleasantries, he pursed his lips and gave me a tight smile. "There's a young doctor; Dr. B is his name, who is just back from some pretty in-depth research and development he was involved with in France. They have developed an innovative surgical technique using some newly invented specialized instruments. His approach is now past the experimental stage, and what he has been able to do suggests to me that we should look into it. There's not a lot of history for this procedure but he doesn't make wild claims. In fact, every little detail of his work has been closely followed and monitored by the AMA. At any rate, I think you should meet with him and see what he has to say."

Wow. Big speech. I already knew I was going to walk. His attitude was guarded optimism. Mine was faith in an all-powerful God. The question still in my mind was whether or not God was going to use doctors for this healing. I felt no firm direction about that in my spirit. I did know that this very nice doctor cared what happened to me.

"Thank you, doctor," I said. "I'll think about it. I'll pray and see what the Lord has to say. You and I have talked a lot over the last months so I'm sure you know I won't make that kind of decision without consulting Him."

One thing this doctor – and almost any doctor – will agree on is the fact that they are helpless to do any healing on their own. Doctors are almost embarrassingly aware that all they can do is kind of lay out the groundwork. Our miraculous bodies – "fearfully and wonderfully made" – do the healing.

"Good," he said. "Do that. If you decide to meet with this doctor, I'll set up an appointment."

As I said, I was conflicted. I really wanted to know exactly how this miracle would happen. God was going to do this. That was for sure. Would I be showing a lack of faith by allowing surgery to get it done? I prayed and although God didn't speak to me audibly at this time, I felt free to meet with this young man.

It was the season I loved. Late fall with winter just around the corner. We had just finished witnessing God wielding His celestial paintbrush as he flung flaming crimson and glowing golds across the landscape. Every year, that glorious fall show seems new to me. Now though, that part was over. All the leaves were gone; the curtain had closed on this year's grand performance. Things looked stark and dry outside. The consolation prize for most of us was that this was the time when families got together for the warmest holidays of the year. I carried an ache in my heart. My family had been dismembered. Thinking back, I thank God for brothers and sisters, nieces and nephews, and my dear sweet faith-filled mom. My entire extended family was a bulwark of support.

My emotions swung from one extreme to the other. Happy – able to experience happiness – one minute, then remembering the enormity of my situation and being blind-sided by sudden remembering…given a figurative slap in the face and having the icy feeling of panic in my belly. Then, looking away from the lies and looking to the Lord and determining to trust Him, but more than that, to thank Him, to praise Him and worship Him. And once again, I would be in that safe place; in the hollow of His hand.

The meeting with the specialist was somewhat less profitable than I had hoped, but I went into it trusting God. It wasn't that I was disrespectful to this young man, though he did look to me like a teen-ager. But I knew and had known for some time that I was the property of the Living God, bought and paid for. There was no need to plead my case or concern myself with whether this nice young doctor was the man for the job or not. I was there to listen – listen to him and also listen for that still small voice that's always trying to give us direction and comfort and wisdom.

He was not so young. Probably in his early thirties and already among the very best in his field. He had a confident, almost cocky air about him. We sat together in his office and after a little small talk, he sat forward, folded his hands and began.

"I have carefully examined all your records. I have given particular attention to the X-rays, CAT scans and MRIs. They tell most of the story, but the effects of the damage done are important to evaluate as well. This beginning paralysis, for example, tells me more than those scans can show."

He got up and came to sit beside me. I wished he hadn't. It hurt to try to turn my head to look to the side. He noticed my discomfort and pulled his chair around so he could face me. "This operation is very difficult," he said. "I am going to be as up-front with you as I possibly can. I see hope for a good outcome for you, but as you know, you must be the one to give the OK. For my part, I am willing to operate. I just want you to be fully aware of the risks involved. Once you know every element of the danger you will be facing, you can make the decision. It's going to be up to you."

"Well," I said, "I came to see you knowing it was not going to be a 'walk in the park.' Until you entered the picture, the expert opinion was that my problem was inoperable. At least you are seeing some kind of a chance. Doctor," I said. "They say I'm looking at life in a wheelchair. I'm a missionary. Maybe God can use a missionary in a wheelchair, but I don't want to live that way. You might not understand when I say this, but God has assured me that I will not be in a wheelchair. I have His promise that I'm going to walk!"

He sat back a little because I had leaned forward as I made that bold statement. "Good," he said. "That confidence can have a lot to do with the outcome."

"How long will the operation take?" I asked.

"It's a long one, Lee Anne, and the length adds a fair amount to the risk. Probably around twelve hours."

"Will it work?…sorry; dumb question. You evidently have some confidence in what you are going to do. How sure are you that it will work?"

I'll give you my guess and that's exactly what it is, a guess; but it's an educated guess. Here it is; you have a 50% chance that we will not have a successful outcome."

"So, 50% chance of success," I said, half wondering why he had not put it in those terms himself. Then I found out.

"Not exactly, Lee Anne," he said. "The probability of success is just 25%. One in four. And it's one in four that you won't survive the operation."

Whoops. This was an interesting situation – for God. Not my problem. I was so peaceful and content to be the cared-for, cared-about child of the King that any risk was His problem. The only question still to be answered was whether or not I would make the decision to go "under the knife."

"I'll let you know soon, Doctor," I said. I left, only a little bemused. *I'll do what you say, Lord,* I prayed.

The next morning at the teacher's meeting, I told everyone about my talk with the doctor. I gave them quite a bit of detail and asked them to pray. I guess what I wanted them to ask God for was some clarity; some more-than-natural wisdom. I didn't have a clear word for myself, but I knew God could bestow faith on anyone for anyone. I also knew that if anyone had faith for instant healing, that would be exactly what would happen. And that "anyone" did not have to be me. "Faith," my brother John says, "Never doesn't work!" I love the simplicity of making it my business to find out what God wants and then going full-speed-ahead on that path. He is so willing to let us know just what His will is. Don't you love that verse; "Be not unwise, but understanding what the will of the Lord is." God never tells us to do anything we are incapable of.

At any rate, I worked with the kind of people that knew how to pray. We had a devotional time every morning. Just being with them and being a part of that spiritual event was like that verse that talks about streams in the desert. Refreshing and spiritually invigorating. They prayed with me then and all of them committed to continue to hold me up before the Lord.

Chapter 31

A little while after that, I was at a staff meeting. Pastor Mac and Lynne Hammond came in as we were wrapping up. The pastor came over to talk. He crouched down next to the easy chair I was sitting in. A man named Bill, one of the teachers' husbands, thoughtfully always tried to provide a comfortable chair. God, bless Bill, please. The very first thing Mac said, after a greeting was, "Tell me about Rory John's accident?" This was strange as Mac followed our high school basketball team and attended a lot of the games. Also, his daughter, Lucyhart was in Rory's class. He had to have known what happened. "Well," I said, "he hit a tree while sledding and snapped his femur. The rod they put in was taken out this summer though, so he'll be fine for the basketball season." Pastor Mac just looked at me. "I know that, Lee Anne," he said. "Just food for thought and a little reminder. Sometimes, when you break a bone you have to have surgery." *Duh*! I thought! *Of course*! This was Pastor Mack Hammond, a man of God well known for his teaching on the miraculous power of God. I pretty much expected him to encourage me to avoid surgery; just get prayer and the laying on of hands. On the other hand, if the operation I was considering was just going to be a simple, straight-forward repair, the question would probably have never come up. I would likely have just gone ahead with it. Prayer would definitely be a component, but standard medical procedures were kind of a given. As it was, since I had been advised of the extreme danger involved, not having the surgery had to be a somewhat logical option. At least, an option to be considered. Pastor Mack surprised me. This man never spoke glibly. He was always thoughtful and careful about any counsel he offered. God used that conversation to give me peace to go ahead and have the surgery. Many years later I met with him in his office. I was scheduled to speak the next night at his church. I asked him if I could share the story. He was interested in what I was going to say. I repeated the scenario and the advice he had so graciously offered me. He looked at me and said, "Boy! I wish I remembered that!" I laughed and asked him if it sounded like something he'd say or did I dream it? He laughed, then and said yes, he very well might have said it. He shook his head in chagrin and said he just felt sorry that something that was that momentous to me had left his memory.

But for this operation, my trust was in the God of my salvation and only in Him. He would be there to provide every needed resource. The outcome would be to His glory. God, and God alone.

I called the doctor and told him I wanted to go ahead. He seemed glad of the decision. I came in and we talked about getting ready.

You may remember the AIDS scare when everyone was worried about infected blood. My own blood was, what they called, "sweet" (Diabetic's blood. Too much sugar) and therefore not usable for anyone else. The doctor asked me to come in ahead of time to give blood that would be stored for the operation. He wanted four pints. One each week. After I had given three, I was too weak to do more. I prayed that three would be enough.

Lee Anne Worre Risk

Chapter 32

December 1, 1991

Mine would be the first time this operation would be performed in the United States.

I'm sure I'm not the only one in the world that gets nervous before having "invasive" surgery. We know they are going to put us out and we won't feel anything during the procedure, but that's part of what bothers us. He had warned me they would have to wake me up midway through the surgery so they could continue with the anesthesia. He assured me I wouldn't remember it, though. I wanted to know what was going to happen. He told me they were videoing the entire process and I could see it afterward.

Maybe I'll go to sleep and never wake up, is a thought that can go through our minds. In a way, we'd kind of like to watch every step. We are always a little bit leery of things being out of our control. The video would have to do.

There are two things that can happen that can cause problems. Well, a lot more than two, I guess. But these two have to do with the anesthesia. They can under-anesthetize you; or they can over-anesthetize you. In that first case, you begin to regain consciousness (and the ability to feel pain) before they have finished cutting and stitching. Their response when they see that happening can be that second thing. A "knee-jerk" reaction which results in you being the recipient of a whole lot more than you ought to have. Too much, of course, can kill you. Neither of these things happens very often, but one of my brothers went through that sequence of events and nearly failed to regain consciousness at all. And who among us, as Christians, would ever enter into an agreement to have surgery without faithful prayer for the whole surgical team. We pray for them all to walk in wisdom, have steady hands and minds clear of distractions. And having done that, we relax and leave everything in the hands of a loving God. Any lingering anxiety is alleviated by that nice warm sleepy feeling that comes from the pre-anesthetic. Having it is nice, but does not, in any way, preclude our need for "The God that Never Sleeps."

So odd to think about this now. I had to be at the hospital at 4:00 AM. It was decided ahead of time that no one should get up that early except the one to drive me there. My driver on this bleak morning was my errant husband. Rory drove a cab and often worked at night. He was the logical choice. I was upset when he arrived to pick me up, and not just because of pre-op nerves. Marta had called; ostensibly to wish me luck. By her tone and by the curt conversation, it seemed to me the call was intended to remind me who Rory was living with. Just hearing her voice made my skin crawl. A rough beginning to what would be a rough day. By the time we got to the hospital, my sugar had taken a nose dive. The symptoms were clear enough and I had enough experience to tell them what was happening.. They took me in quickly and started a glucose IV before I went into diabetic shock. They told Rory he could come in. When he did, he kissed me on the forehead, told me he loved me and walked out. He did not stay for the surgery. Anissa came with the other two kids at 6:00.

Everybody knew how terribly dangerous this surgery was going to be. My kids all got around me there in the pre-op room and fervently prayed the prayer of faith. Then, during the surgery while I would be "out of it" and not be continuing in conscious prayer, they would be keeping a prayer vigil. My family are a group of praying people. I was comfortable knowing they were praying even though I knew they might not stay the whole time. The surgeon came in to check on me and waited quietly at the door till the prayers were over. When we were done, he walked over to the foot of the bed and solemnly clasped his hands. He was dressed for surgery in a green outfit and his mask dangled from his neck.

"This is a big day, Lee Anne," he said. "You know the risks we face. I say we, because we see those risks as ours as well as yours. Your attitude going in to this is an important part of the potential for success. Especially in the recovery phase. I just want to tell you that for us, our whole team, this is not routine; not at all. Every one of us is intent on doing our very best. We will do everything possible to produce an excellent result." He looked around the room. "I know you were praying for me; for us. Thank you."

I began to feel the calming effects of the pre-anesthesia and sleepily said a slightly slurred "See you later" and was wheeled down the corridor to the surgical suite. When I was later told about what went on in that operating room, I was glad I had not been conscious and aware.

They brought me in and once I was all the way under the anesthetic, they moved me to a special table. I was strapped tightly and they could then rotate me as if I were on a rotisserie. I was opened up, first from the front; then rotated to where I was face down and could be opened up from the back. My organs had to be removed and taken out of the way without being detached so they could be tucked back into place when the surgery was over. They rested in pans on a table situated right next to the rest of me. Part of the process involved taking plugs of bone from the bones that made up my hips. Those are larger in surface and can be "cored" without losing too much integrity. Those bone plugs were used to re-create sections of spine. A good many screws and pins would insure many, many delays at airport screenings.

During a grueling twelve and a half hours, I was cut into, re-arranged, tilted so I could drain, and once, I died, strapped to that table. I guess I don't have to tell you I didn't stay dead. Nobody ever gave me any idea of how long my heart was not beating, but my brain seems to work okay. At least as good as the average Norwegian. We Norwegians are a tough bunch. They revived me, finished doing what they were in the process of doing, put me back together, sewed me up and then, brought me to recovery. I was kept in intensive care for several days on a morphine drip. I began to wake up when they took me off that and moved me to a regular room. I came back into the world and to a fresh understanding and relationship with pain. Yes, I hurt a lot, but I felt good at the same time, if that makes any sense.

They re-fitted me for another form fit body cast. It was like the one I had had before, but was designed and made to fit and support me as perfectly as could be. Without it, I wouldn't be able to begin to sit up and practice walking again.

I was released from the hospital on December twenty fourth, Christmas eve. I had pushed for my release and had pretended I was better than I actually was. Physically, it was probably way too soon. In my spirit, being home with my family around me gave me peace.

The doctor pronounced the surgery a success. I think he wrote a paper for the medical journals. If he got some acclaim for his work, I'm happy. They did use the video of the operation for training purposes for quite some time afterward. My doctor told me it would not be such a great idea for me to watch it. Maybe I'll see it on the discovery channel sometime. I'm really not that curious. The path ahead of me was clear. All I needed to do was begin the months of healing and therapy. I would walk!

Chapter 33

Once in a while, someone will ask if I ever thought about getting married again. It is a good, logical question to ask. For someone as crippled up as I was, a husband would surely be helpful to have around. Ministry teams always seemed to have more effectiveness. As the Word so aptly puts it; "Two are better than one for they will have a reward for their labor. If one falls, he (or she) will have another to pick him (or her) up." Very apt, in my case. Not that I was falling down all the time, but you get the idea.

During that time of getting stronger and healing, there were two men at two different times that seemed to care for me. I was pretty skittish about any kind of romantic relationship and told them both as much. Both felt that surely God would want me to have someone in my life that would take care of me. They tried to give me good reasons for marrying. I made sure they knew how strongly I felt about my calling to the mission field. Their idea was that I could still go on missions trips when I got better and maybe I could also be effective by serving on church missions boards. Wouldn't that please the Lord? It was hard to say no. There it was, right in front of me. I knew God often directed by creating circumstances that push us one way or the other. Was this what was going on here? I began to seek the Lord in prayer. If I had learned anything through all this, it was that God has a detailed plan for each of us and I wanted desperately to find and follow His plan for me.

I was so tired, by then, of the seemingly unending struggle to be strong. I was still on this earth for my children; Jesus had made that point back in the hospital that awful day. I felt the responsibility of being strong for them. The pain was a constant that wore me down physically and emotionally. Just to wake up and get out of bed in the morning was a daily challenge. I was still battling the temptation to believe I would be better off dead. But the God who kept me going, the God who loved me with an undying love, the God whose love would not let me go was there and knew every hardship and all the pain I was enduring. What should I do?

Finally, I quit beating around the bush and straight out asked Him.

We say; "If life gives you lemons, make lemonade." For us as Christians, I believe that God will make something good out of our honest mistakes if our heart's intent is to please Him. We talk about God's permissive will as opposed to His perfect will. Speaking from experience, there have been times when I just didn't want to do what it felt like God was telling me to do. I would do what I wanted and comfort myself with the thought that God would bless it anyway. Make me some lemonade. Maybe that can happen.

A few weeks went by and I began to feel the Lord begin to answer. He didn't speak audibly this time, but I felt a strong sense of His presence and direction. I felt, clearly, that He was telling me it was all right if I wanted to get married. I could end the struggle, become the suburban housewife and have someone to take care of me. I heard Him and then heard more. He was saying that He had a larger plan for me and if I was able to wait, following that direction would result in far greater glory for Him and far more satisfaction for me.

In Paul's letter to the Roman church, he talks about God's call on a person's life. The eleventh chapter; verse twenty nine he says; "For the gifts and calling of the Lord are irrevocable." In the Amplified; "He never withdraws them when once they are given, and He does not change His mind about those to whom He gives His grace or to whom He sends His call." Pretty clear. Pretty emphatic. From that I have to understand that if we had a call, (and there is nothing more sure to me that we did.) I was not released from that call just because my husband jumped the tracks and went off in another direction. I was called and I knew it. I was alive. I was willing to be used. I only needed to put one foot in front of the other and walk. By His grace and with His anointing, I would do what He wanted me to do.

Whenever you can, dear reader, opt for His perfect will for your life. I decided to wait upon the Lord, renew my strength, and mount up with wings like an eagle. So I did.

Chapter 34

I am writing this in the year 2016. More than 25 years have elapsed since that tumultuous time took place. There is a lot to tell you about what has happened in my life during that time. For one thing; it sure went by in a hurry. More than two and a half decades and it seems like a blur.

As you, of course, know by now, God kept me going. To start with, He sent me back to the scene of the crime. Interesting that He wanted me in a place where my humiliation had been so apparent. What purpose was there in keeping me in a place that held so much in the way of painful memories? He did that to my dismay…and against my advice. Of course, His purpose was perfect. I just didn't see it at first.

The catalyst was a plan to go down and open up a Christian coffee house. It sounded fun to me. And who was I to try to avoid the embarrassment of being where all my old acquaintances could see me?

I saw myself acting as a kind of lady deacon…making good coffee, baking cookies, serving tables and cleaning up after people. That would be necessary work and certainly God-honoring. I knew

I could be content in that role. There would be someone else to do the actual ministry stuff, I was sure.

It didn't happen that way. Not exactly, anyway.

It did start out like that. We got the little coffee shop up and running. The Mexican fellow who was to be my partner took over and kind of re-purposed the whole thing. His idea was to have a kind of hang-out for Christians. He didn't want the rough crowd around. That was okay, but not for me. I believed God called me to reach the lost, not coddle the found. Maybe a little too harsh there, and turning it into a little fellowship group might have been fine, just not what I felt I was sent to do at that time. I did perfect some great recipes for baked goods. All these years later, my brownies and carrot cake are still being avidly consumed all around the area. My former partner and his family have made it a profitable little business.

Right away, I also began to work with three local churches. My experience with kids and young people made me a welcome addition to the volunteer staff at each one. I was serving unpaid, of course. I was happy. The trauma to the local body caused by Rory's behavior was being amended by my presence and the healing power of the Holy Spirit. The whole mess was well known, but people were seeing that God was bigger and relationships were being restored.

Someone who was a part of one of those three churches had a government position as head of the prisons in our state. He came to me and asked if I would organize Bible studies in those places. I started in a women's prison and ended up helping in five prisons in all. From time to time, an American female would be arrested – usually for some crime involving drugs - and they would call me for help in translating for these girls. Almost always, they had come down from the states with a boyfriend with the idea of making a big drug buy and going back to sell it for big money. Typically, they were not too smart. They always thought they were though, till they were caught.

Thinking back, I guess there may have been some danger of violent behavior from the more hardened criminals. The prison staff and guards were attentive to the surroundings though, and we were not left alone until we had a good sized group meeting each week. Nothing ever happened to threaten us on our visits. The influence of the gospel did good things for those convicts who heard and believed. Overall, the prisons became more manageable with the introduction and acceptance of the Word of God. That ministry bore fruit. I was happy.

We heard about an orphanage in a city not too far away and went to see what we could do to help. There were about 35 children living in the worst imaginable conditions. The building was falling down around them and those kids were eating sparsely, were wearing ragged clothing and some were in very poor health. Even in those conditions, the ladies who ran the place kept it immaculately clean. Quite a feat. That old saw reworked for Mexico is usually "Cleanliness is next to impossible." There was a table in the dining room, but you could eat off the floor. We became ambassadors of the Lord Jesus to that squalid place. We made routine trips to bring food and help. We often were able to bring in medical and work teams. You can imagine what a literal God-send that was. After all this time, we are still in contact with some of them.

My youngest, Katy, had gotten to know a young Mexican named Horacio Garay. He was in law school and she was at Christ for the Nations in Dallas. Lots of long-distance phone calls and lengthy bus rides to see each other made theirs an expensive courtship. They were married in 1997 and began Bible studies and prayer meetings held in my living room there in Zacatecas. Those little home meetings became the foundation for a church. They called it "Roca Eterna" Eternal Rock; also translated as "Rock of Ages." It grew and God used it. Still does.

Today, it is situated in a large warehouse-like building that also houses a thriving Christian school. As I write this, more than sixty kids attend. Katy and Horacio have seven children of their own. Their kids were the original student body and the reason for it all. The classes are all taught in English. Mexican families love the idea that their children could get this kind of "leg up" through that school.

Around the same time that Roca Eterna was being formed, we began to see the need for an orphanage there in Zacatecas. For years, we had worked to help the orphanage in Morelia. When people came down on missions trips, we would make the eight hour drive to bring workers and helpers. "Uncle Ted" Kjeseth, gone to be with Jesus now and eighty years old at the time, had a team of retired men who called themselves "Craftsmen for Christ." Those good men performed near miracles at the Morelia orphanage. Morelia street orphans survived because of the warm climate there. In Zacatecas, any child out in the elements stood a good chance of pneumonia or worse unless they could find shelter.

People talked and word got around that there was a place those little strays could be taken. Horacio's mom and dad became a depository for those little ones. Their house had limited space and, thanks to help from a foundation formed by the Peters family, we got a building that became "Casa Hogar" a place of safety.

One day during those early times, a young couple came to us with their tiny little nearly five-year-old boy. They had come from a mountain tribe sixteen hours from Zacatecas. They had brought their little boy because there were plans to sacrifice him; murder him, on his fifth birthday. The little boy's grandfather was a Shaman; a witchdoctor who had issued the direction to do this awful thing. The boy's uncle had gotten saved and, with his family had escaped the tribe. We were aghast at the story and of course, took him in

He was terrified of us and of everything he saw. His life had been truly primitive before he came to us and electricity, running water, every kind of appliance scared him to death. It's hard to know what went through his mind when he saw a toilet flush, but that made him hysterical with fear. We couldn't communicate at all since he knew only his tribal dialect. For three weeks, we struggled to make ourselves understood and then; Veggie Tales! That wonderful animated series produced in the Spanish language created the bridge for communication and the basis for him to learn Spanish. Along with five other orphans that grew up with us, that once frightened little boy is in college today.

You might think we could take as many orphans as we saw fit. It seems logical that any kind of shelter for homeless kids is better than leaving them out on the street. Logic, however, has never been a match for bureaucracy. We are limited to just sixteen children under current laws. We get several requests every week to take more. We need to expand and all we need are the funds to do that. This ministry is so worthy of support. It is so gratifying to literally see, first hand what God is doing with the money given by faithful Christians.

Another amazing outreach God put on our hearts is the now annual production of a powerful Christian musical drama called "The Gospel According to Scrooge." It was first written and produced in the states and for years, churches all over the country and around the English speaking world put it on and saw many thousands of people brought to Christ through its' message.

We saw it as a perfect way to reach out to the city at large and assumed the difficult task of translating it into Spanish. This musical has swelled to large proportions and multiple performances are packed to the rafters. Hundreds raise their hands for prayer at the invitation given at the end of each performance. The Mexican people love drama and music. This is almost irresistible to them.

A number of years ago, I was invited to a missions conference being held at a big church in Long Island, New York. The pastor there, a kind and powerful man of God named Bob Forseth, had heard about some of the trials of Lee Anne Risk. He gently but firmly insisted that my story needed to be told. I demurred, just as firmly insisting that speaking wasn't what I felt led to do. He won that argument and I found myself in the prayer room in front of around forty people, gasping and crying through a twenty minute version of my testimony. I have given my testimony hundreds of times since and you would think I could get used to it to the point where I could hold back my emotions, but I still find myself gasping and crying; talking in a high, squeaky voice through particularly difficult parts of it. When I cry, I squeak. I just can't help it.

My story is one of redemption and restoration. I have been given His life to pour out and I can say with all confidence that my God can take the least likely candidate and if that one will surrender to His will, miracles will happen. I know you will understand that when someone tells me they can't do it – whatever it is – it makes me crazy. We call ourselves believers. If we are, we'd better believe. The Word does not say; "I can do a few things through Christ which strengthens me."

Are we all called to the same calling? No.

Are we all called to listen and obey and give testimony to the power and love of God? Surely this is true!

People often tell me that they aren't called to be a missionary. I know what they mean, but their understanding is wrong! We're all called. On that, there really can be no argument and few Christians would disagree. God put no qualifiers to His mandate, "Go Ye". He just said "Go". Get a move on! Maybe not all to a foreign field, but certainly to our neighbors and families. Every single child of God redeemed by His blood has a testimony. Share it with your life and like St Francis of Assisi wrote, "Preach the gospel at all times and when necessary, use words."

Yes. I urge and encourage every follower of the Lord Jesus Christ to touch the things of this world lightly. Taking a firm hold on those things can create a bond. Bonds bind. Keep this thought available to your consciousness. Anything that holds a place in your attention or affection that's higher than the place you've given the Lord is an idol. Every believer has the opportunity to be mightily used of God. If my life and experience are of any use, it would be that Christ in me – not me alone – Christ in me and correspondingly, Christ in you brings Jesus to visible life here on this earth.

Lee Anne Worre Risk

"Go into all the world." Jesus' last instructions. Such a grand idea. So hard to realize personally. So hard to even visualize.

Let me give you an example of how God can bless and anoint our efforts when we follow His lead.

Roland Ashby, who had introduced me to the orphanage in Morelia, started a youth outreach called "Terremoto Juvenil" or "Youthquake" in English. Ten days each summer when 400-500 kids came together from the USA and Mexico to work together, play together, eat together, etc. The first 5 days we were in a camp setting where they were put into teams and taught skits, mimes, and personal evangelism. Then the next 5 days they were sent out all over central Mexico to hook up with local churches and do street ministry. I was a kind of kitchen supervisor, menu coordinator, cook and I purchased the groceries. They consumed a lot of food!

It was a very effective outreach! Thousands of lives were changed and touched through it. Each year there were hundreds of decisions for Christ! There are so many that we know of today that are in full time ministry and attribute their time with Terremoto with opening their hearts and minds to hear the call of the Lord. Only in heaven will we know the whole story.

We had come to know a remarkable young man by the name of Marcos Witt. Marcos was the son of missionaries and his father had been martyred; murdered at the hands of the very people he was trying to reach with the gospel. (Quite an amazing story in itself; told in the book, "The Foolishness of God" written by Mark's mother, Nola Warren.)

This amazing young man was gifted by the Lord in music. When we first met, he was already one of the most popular and well-known singers in the Spanish speaking world. Even though his music was focused on the Lord and on worship of the King of Kings, Marcos was featured on many secular radio stations and on television as well. He and his production company, CanZion, have won dozens of Grammys in the years since.

God had given Marcos Witt a vision for a particular kind of ministry that would impact all of Latin America. He called me and asked if we could meet and talk. I was intrigued. We got together.

Over coffee and cookies, Marcus began to describe what he believed God had given him to do.

"A school, Lee Anne," he said, leaning forward in his chair, his voice quiet, but intense. "We started last semester here in Durango. We will train young people to be praise and worship leaders. And, at the same time they'd get complete Bible/ministry school courses, too! They'd be real music ministers! Once they have completed their studies, these students will be prepared to go start churches or, at least add support to existing congregations."

"Imagine," he enthused. "There is nothing like this in all of Latin America!"

I was enthralled. What a wonderful idea! There was no doubt in my mind that this was a "last days" concept that was birthed by God.

"I am so excited and thrilled to hear this, Marcos," I said. "Thank you for taking this time to tell me about it. Can I help in any way? I will surely spread the word to everyone we work with. Maybe we can add to the number of students."

He smiled. "Of course, Lee Anne, but I need you in a more direct way. God put you in my mind. Will you consider being involved in the school itself?"

I was taken aback. There surely were more capable people than me. Definitely others more qualified. I was embarrassed at the thought that he had, somehow, gotten the impression that I was a lot more than I was. For a moment, I just sat there.

I said, "Do you need someone to teach English?" That was all I could imagine he wanted.

"Lee Anne," he said, "I want you to take the position of Dean of women."

I sat back and uttered a short laugh. "Oops. Not funny. Excuse me," I said.

He chuckled in response. "Nope, not funny, very serious, and I hope you will see this as God's idea, not mine. Not that I wouldn't choose you for this position on my own. God sent me here to talk to you today."

"You want me to move to Durango"? My mind was reeling. I had just recently gotten so busy in Zacatecas.

"Yes," he said. "That is my thought."

Oh, my.

Well, I began to explain about the orphanage and the prisons, the churches and youth groups where I was working. And, in so doing, shared what God had been teaching me regarding missions.

"I've lived all these years with one kind of vision, Mark, but God is opening my mind and heart and showing me that it's time Latin Americans get involved in missions too. They've been on the receiving end of things for many years and they seem like perfect choices to go to the Middle East. There is such a terrible need."

I continued to try to explain what my heart was aching for.

"Up till now, America and Europe have been sending most of the missionaries. Just lately, Argentina and Brazil have begun to do their part. I want to see our Latino Christians catch the vision and the passion for those lost souls: Muslims, Buddhists, Hindus. And there are still many tribal peoples, some right here in Mexico, that have never yet heard the name of Jesus...not one time. I feel so strongly that this is the last frontier in reaching 'the ends of the earth'," and I believe the Lord wants Latinos to be a big part of it."

I can't remember exactly all I said, but I'm sure I went on and on. I can really get going when I speak about the need for missionaries!

His face suddenly lit up.

"Okay. I get it. Yes, the Lord surely did put you on my heart but now I see why. It is because we need a Dean of Missions!" He threw back his head and laughed. "You can start anytime."

My heart was beating fast and adrenalin flowed. We talked more and more with his wife, Miriam adding ideas and details as well. Soon, we had formed a basic plan and had set up some goals for this new department of missions. I began to spend a week each month at the school in Durango. We held missions conferences each semester. We directed our students toward involvement in the local churches and even started doing some short term outreaches. We also sent a small team led by my dear friends, Paul and Kathy Cagle, to Spain where they passed out Spanish Bibles for those who took the ferry to Morocco, where so many Spanish speaking Muslims cross daily.

It started there in Durango and grew…and grew…and grew. At one time there were students who had come from 28 countries! It became more and more difficult to get those foreign students into

Mexico so the Lord put it on the hearts of some staff and students to take this wonderful idea to their home countries. The next school opened in Argentina where today there are eleven schools. Then came a school in Paraguay. At around this time, Marcos was called to a large church in Houston to pastor. That led to opening a school there. From there the need to open in other places around the world became apparent. Central America and more of South America including Brazil. Then our Spain and Portugal schools provided opportunities to opening schools in Africa. Today, these schools - called CanZion Institutes – are located all over the world. The total is now nearing eighty as I write this. The last grand opening I got to attend was in Mozambique, Africa. Imagine! Me! I got to attend one of the missions schools! These two schools (one other in Guinea Bissau) were started and staffed by our own people and totally supported by our schools all over the world. I cried the whole first 3 days. God used two young gals, graduates from Mexico and from Argentina, to get that school open.

Miraculous! One student shared how he walked all the way through three countries to get there. He wanted to learn and then take it back home to teach others in his country. It brings tears again as I write these words. They were willing.

I have acted as the head of missions and as the head of counseling. I have taught classes in methods of Bible study. I have traveled the world. I did it! I went out "into all the world." When I stop to think of what has gone on, I almost feel like I'm dreaming.

Did I need to undergo such trauma and heartache in order for my experience to inspire and challenge others? It might be the right thing for some to read and hear, and maybe the story can be shared - to be read or heard by others whose hearts might be touched. God often uses what I think of as a "ripple effect" to spread the information He wants people to hear. There is no question that many others have been used in far greater ways than I without having to go through the kind of pain I have endured. It sounds corny, but, like Paul, I say my experience is nothing compared to what my Lord endured on my behalf. So, please do not take my story to mean that God will put you through tremendous agony before you become usable. Jesus takes a mess and makes a miracle. That's what he does. He has different plans for each of us. You might not need to be put through the wringer like I was, but you do have to die; to "lose your life". But you already knew that.

As I come to the conclusion of this story, my heart yearns for you, dear reader, to open your heart and mind to the tremendous life God has planned for you. I am praying for you. Just keep it simple and take God at His word. Great things will follow. Was it Dwight Moody who said, and I paraphrase; "The world has yet to see what can happen when a man (or woman) is completely sold out to God?"

Lee Anne Worre Risk

The time is short.
The fields are white.
Who will go and work in the fields?

The End

The name of the book
comes from an old hymn, actually.
The words are amazing.

Love that will not let me go

O Love that wilt not let me go,
I rest my weary soul in thee;
I give thee back the life I owe,
That in thine ocean depths its flow
May richer, fuller be.

O light that foll'west all my way,
I yield my flick'ring torch to thee;
My heart restores its borrowed ray,
That in thy sunshine's blaze its day
May brighter, fairer be.

O Joy that seekest me through pain,
I cannot close my heart to thee;
I trace the rainbow through the rain,
And feel the promise is not vain,
That morn shall tearless be.

O Cross that liftest up my head,
I dare not ask to fly from thee;
I lay in dust life's glory dead,

And from the ground there blossoms red
Life that shall endless be.

Lee Anne Worre Risk

A letter from Rory

(This letter gives Rory's side of what took place. He is forthright in telling it and hopeful his experience will help others choose wisdom when life choices are made.)

When Marta came to work for us, I saw a young, pretty girl with a shy and quiet way about her. I liked what I saw. When it became apparent to me that she looked at me with hopeful eyes and that there was a certain spark of attraction between us, a door opened. I looked the other way for a time, but the door was there, beckoning. I went through that door.

I was an only child. My father was old-school Lebanese: my mother, a pretty Swede. Our home was a Christian home. My folks were born-again. I was brought up in an atmosphere of love and was nurtured according to Godly ways. I was spoiled, I guess, but not by being given money and toys. My folks weren't wealthy. I was indulged by rarely being told no. It was we three against the world. I felt special and I loved my life back then.

Lee Anne Worre Risk

My mother got sick with cancer and died while I was just in my teens. I loved my mother very much. I couldn't understand why God would let her die like that. My dad and I both had a very hard time because of losing her. We both continued to go to church regularly. Our lives kind of revolved around our church family. The pastor had a daughter and she was attracted to my dad. She helped fill a void in his life, I guess, and just a year after my mother died, they were married. It was awkward for me as his new wife was barely older than I was. The late teens are a time when every young man encounters all kinds of life-altering experiences. My life was a tumultuous whirlwind. Beyond the normal changes of graduating from high school, getting into the much higher stress of college, beginning to become a man; but still a boy, I faced the world with bravado and at the same time, some apprehension. The three had become two; dad and I, and now with his new wife and a life of his own, there was one. Me. I was on my own.

I wish I could say that it was still two; that God and I walked into the unknown future together, but it didn't feel that way. I know God was there, but I didn't acknowledge his presence or help. Thanks to my unstructured upbringing, I continued my foot-loose – no boundaries – life-style. Most of my friendships had formed as far back as grade school. Our gang was made up, mostly, of kids from church. Looking back, I am grateful for the way the family of God kept me in check. Things could so easily have gotten much further out of hand sooner, otherwise. However, like those people in the Bible, I did what was right in my own eyes. The gang, for the most part, did the same. If someone had asked me if I was a Christian, I would have said I was, but I was pretty casual about it.

I had a few semi-serious relationships with the opposite sex, but then I started going out with Lee Anne. She liked me and I liked that she liked me. I wanted to be loved; not so strange a desire. Everybody wants to be loved and to be needed.

I went into the armed services, but was given a medical discharge after a pretty brief stint. High blood pressure, they said. That was okay with me. Those people were a bossy bunch.

I tried college for a bit. I was probably more interested in what I had heard about college life than about the education. I was a pretty good athlete and college sports looked like fun. College dorm parties and that whole scene sounded good too. I lasted a year at the University of Minnesota. Staying in college was going to involve some scholastic effort, it seemed. I wasn't in the mood.

There is that thing people refer to as "Every man's battle." When you are in your teens, raging hormones make it a losing fight a lot of the time. Even if a guy doesn't go around having sex with every possible candidate, most guys during those years are having all they can, at least, in their imaginations. It started at puberty, and never let up. I was always on the hunt; always looking for that returning, inviting look from any attractive female I came across. I got through high school and even my brief college career without actually succeeding at what I truly wanted to do. From Jesus's perspective, of course, I was as guilty as I could be, having looked at scores of women with lust in my heart. Many encounters and many near-successes marked the path through my life up till we got married.

I would love to say that my battle was over once I had a loving wife and had begun a family. Such was not the case. I continued to struggle with a "wandering eye." I prayed fervently. I wanted to be satisfied, but I was tormented by thoughts and fantasies. I would push those thoughts away, but it was never long before my mind allowed them to return. On the surface, it probably looked as if everything was fine. I was the quintessential hypocrite – acting like I was a good husband and father while these uncontrolled impulses raged inside me. Satan was having a field day and my flesh was a willing accomplice.

God called us to His work. Amazing, that He would take someone as badly flawed as I was, but, somehow, He used me. He does that. He'll take the foolish to confound the wise. I'm not sure now, but part of the reason He might have been able to use me was because I felt so unusable. I know there are a lot of God's children that don't get much done for the kingdom. Sometimes the reason is something called "spiritual pride." We read the Bible, study to show ourselves approved, pray every day (concentrating on the needs and faults of others, usually) and generally see ourselves as spiritually superior. When we get to that place, we fundamentally block the work of the Holy Spirit. The problem is, we have a hard time seeing our error. We feel so spiritual.

I had a very clear idea of what a mess I was. Maybe I was empty enough that the Lord could fill me and He, Himself could get something done. God needs us to be empty vessels.

At any rate, I was able to pray with desperate souls, counsel (with Godly wisdom, I always hoped,) and recognized in myself a God-given ministry of encouragement. I preached when the need arose, but never felt it was my main calling. Mexico felt good and right…and, so crazy, my eye still wandered.

From the outset, I knew it was wrong. I felt helpless in trying to shake it off. In order to entertain any thoughts of perpetrating a relationship with Marta, I had to turn off my mind, turn away and refuse to acknowledge the truth. So, that's what I did.

There were a number of reasonable, rational excuses for becoming involved. She was the damsel in distress; I was the knight in shining armor, coming to her rescue. Her husband was abusive. When he got drunk, she was beaten and came to work with bruises. He took her little bit of money to buy beer and cigarettes. So much injustice. She needed a protector. I stepped right in.

A good friend from Minnesota, Curtis Frankhauser, had become a minister. He got word to us that he was coming to Mexico and would be in Monterrey at a certain time. Marta and I had become seriously entangled by then and I had enough sense to know I should do something to try to end it. I drove to Monterrey, praying all the way. My intent was to see my friend and to tell him what was happening. I wanted to get help and counsel. Instead, I spent a couple of days with him, talked for hours about everything but what I had gone there to talk about. My intentions had been clear and serious. During that two days, there had been a number of times when I could have broached the subject. Every time I got ready to bring it up, something would close my mouth. Pride, shame, maybe rebellion. But my plan never came to be.

Curtis left for Minnesota and I drove back to Zacatecas – a kind of hopeless, fatalistic feeling in my heart. I wasn't happy. I was ashamed. I was going back to a life of secrecy and deception. I was careful not to let my thoughts become too clear. I knew if I did, I couldn't live with myself.

I have learned since, that one good way to deal with temptation effectively is to play out the entire outcome of giving in to it. It's not too hard to sort of forecast the consequences of your actions; your decision to sin. It's actually pretty easy. You just have to ask yourself what the long-term effects of this activity will be? You also have to really want to know.

Too often, we "sacrifice the permanent on the altar of the immediate". Like Moses, enjoying the pleasures of sin for a season.

We just don't think too hard about it and lie to ourselves about how, afterwards we will go to the Lord for forgiveness. How foolish to believe that God will wink at our folly (His love is unconditional, we tell ourselves) and we won't be forced to reap the disgusting crop that springs up with such healthy alacrity. But that's exactly what we want to believe.

I know Lee Anne loved me and was contented with a life as a helpmate. She was the ideal missionary's wife. She organized and cooked, worked with the women and children, and, I know, held me up in prayer.

Me? I was not content. I should have been. God was faithful and was providing a fruitful field for us in which to labor. If I had been content and not selfishly thinking of myself alone, I would have "kept my eye on the prize" as Paul put it instead of allowing it to wander. I loved Lee Anne and I loved my kids. It may be hard to understand what I did, knowing that. What it boils down to is this. I had been rehearsing for this role for most of my adult life. My thoughts and fantasies laid the groundwork for everything that happened. Marta happened to come along at a point in my life when I was primed for the occasion. She presented an opportunity. I took it.

I don't believe I lost my salvation or a home in heaven because of what I did. So much else was lost and gone forever, though. Was my primary motive and concern to do what was best for Marta? Or was I simply being selfish and self-indulgent? To be as honest as I can, I have to admit that my own desires and satisfaction were the dominant factors. That dumb Debby Boone song with the line, "This can't be wrong if it feels so right" is a self-justifying rationale that works fine if you don't hold it up against the truth of God's Word. I remember trying to explain it to my brother-in-law. "Can you imagine what it would be like to have someone believe you are the most wonderful thing in the world – someone that treated you like the sun rose and set on you? That's what it's like with Marta," I told him.

He sat across from me, a sad and skeptical look on his face. He wasn't about to agree with me. In fact, he told me that what I was doing was tragic. He told me later that he could understand it a little, but still had to call it a tragedy. I guess I have to agree. When I try to make sense of it, my mind goes in circles.

64834331R00141

Made in the USA
Lexington, KY
21 June 2017